To: ______________________

From: ______________________

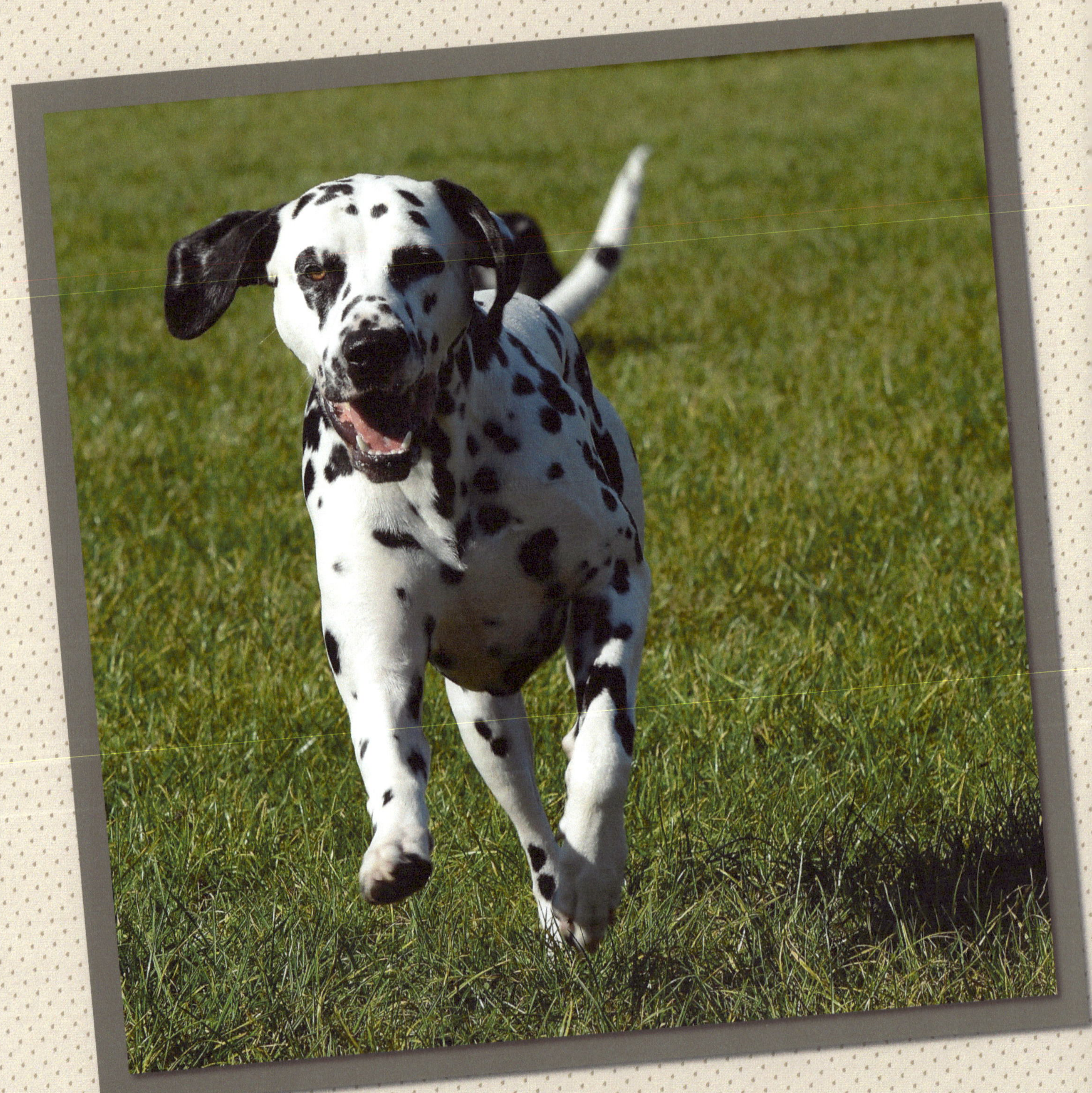

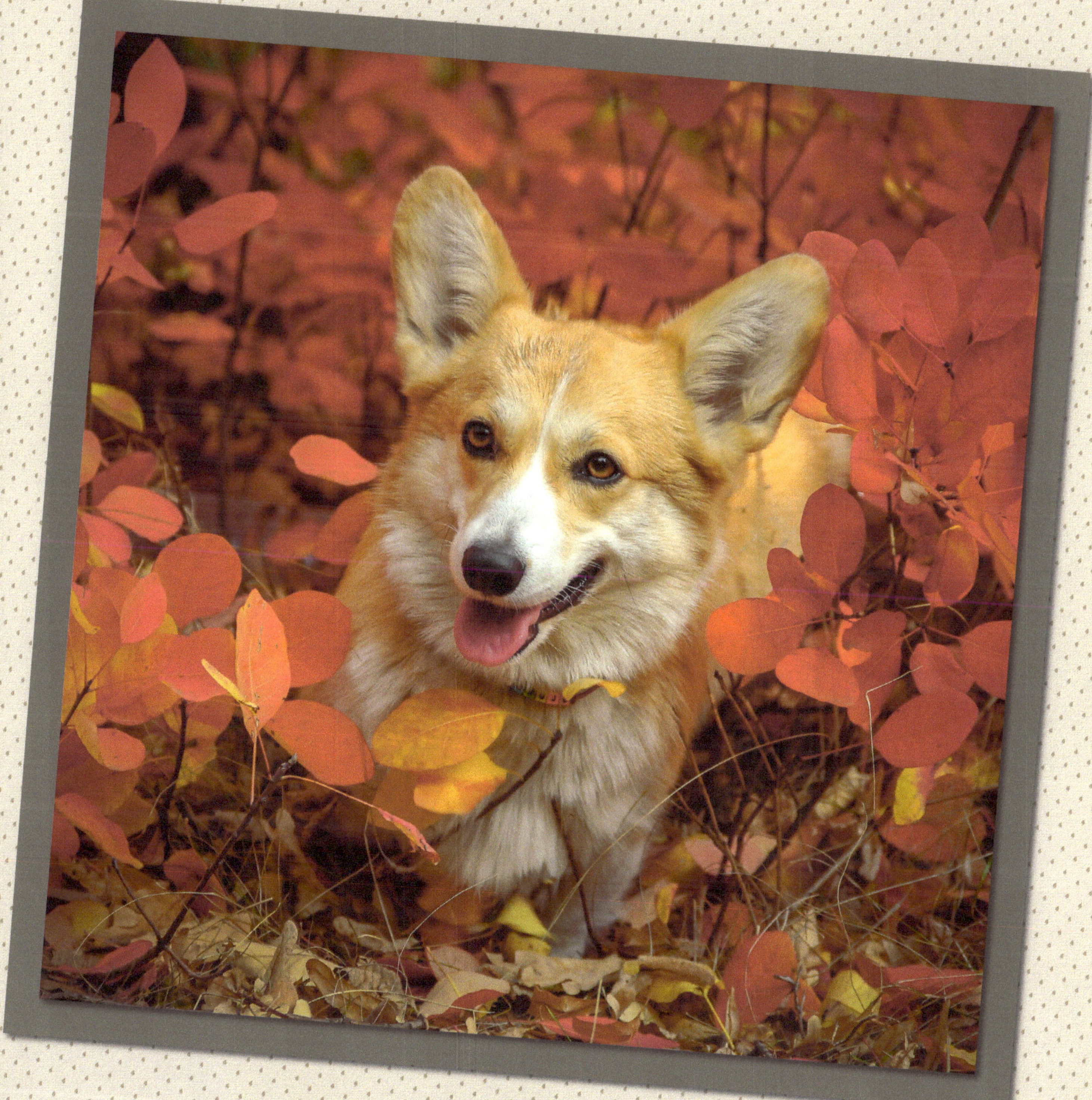

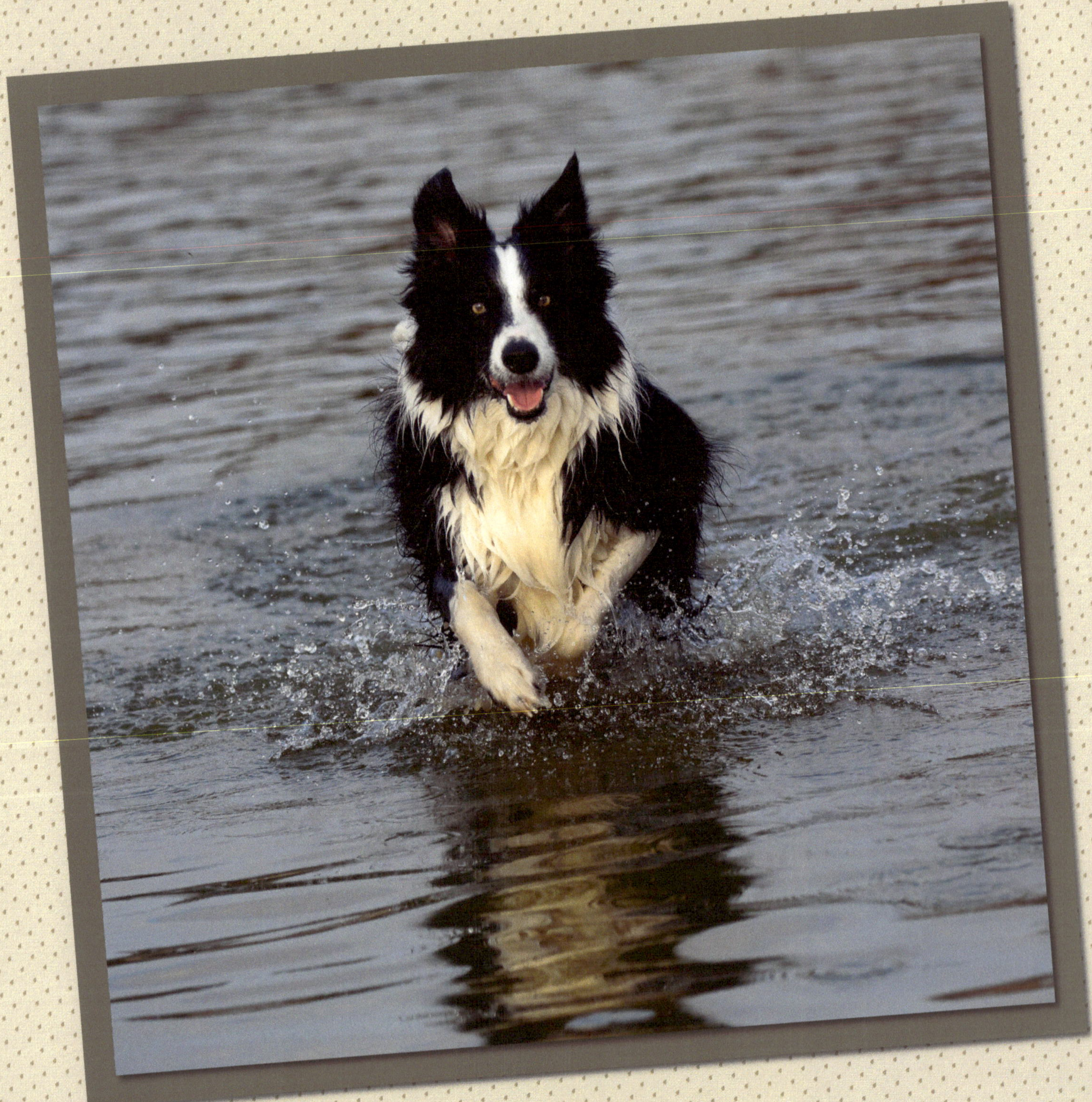

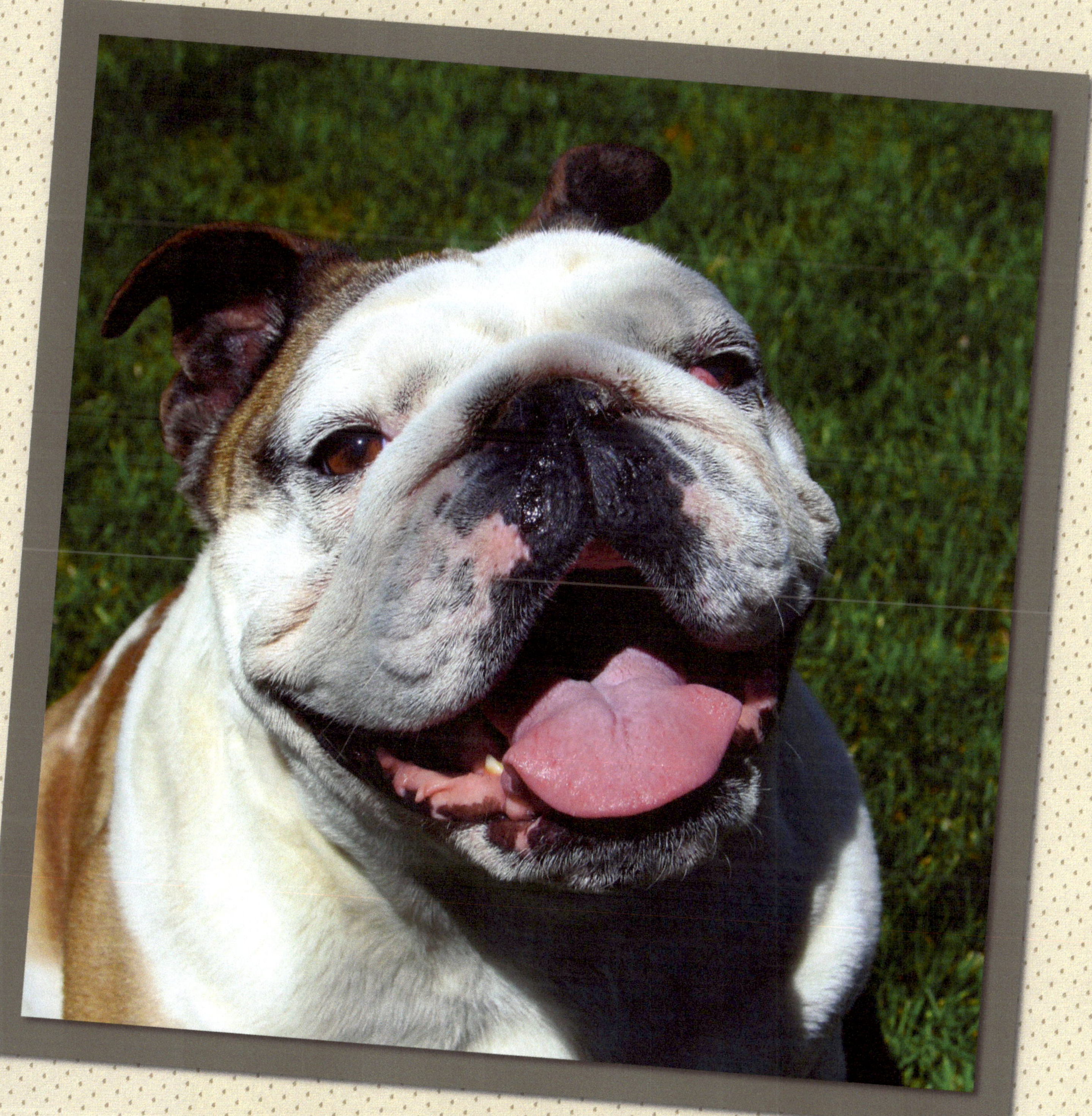

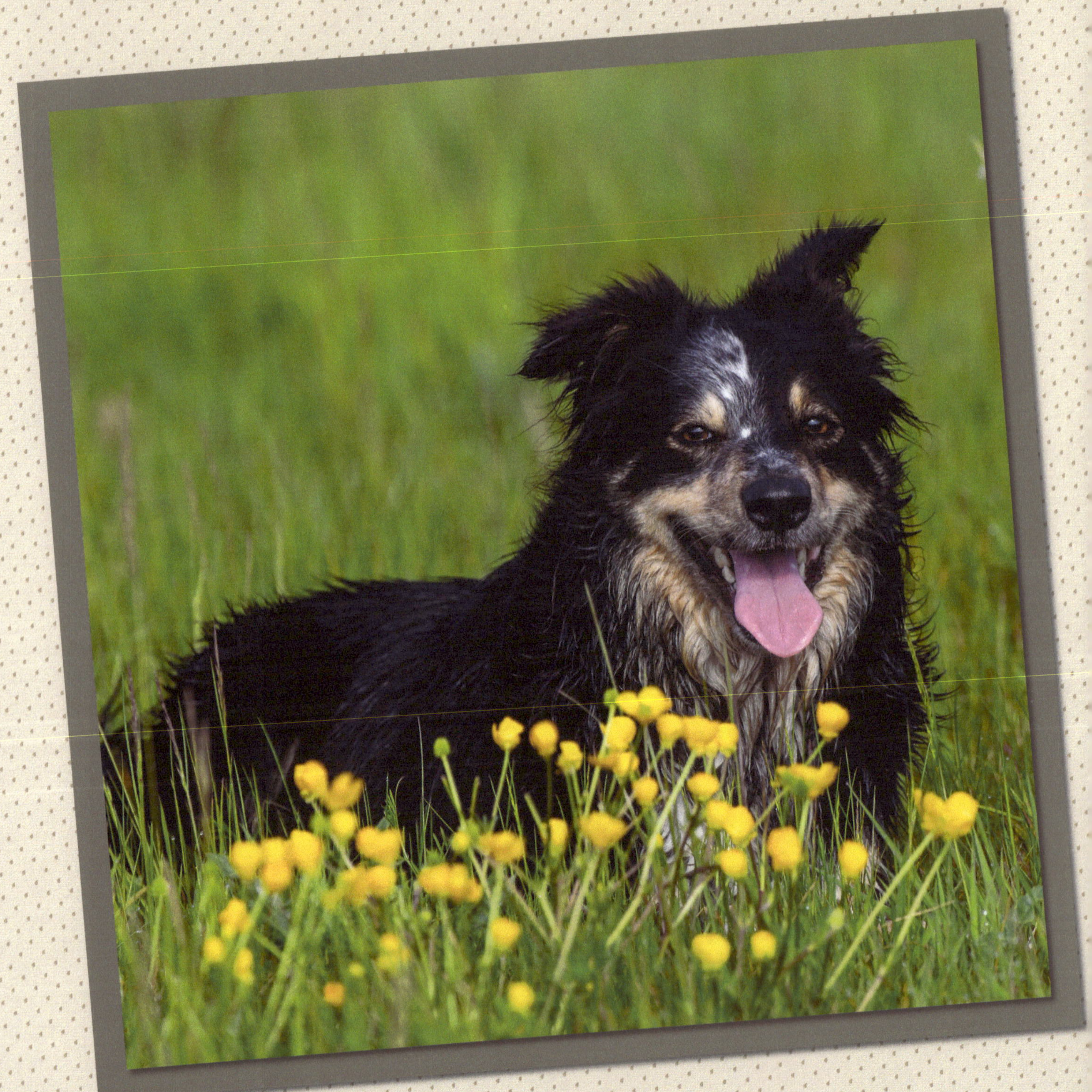

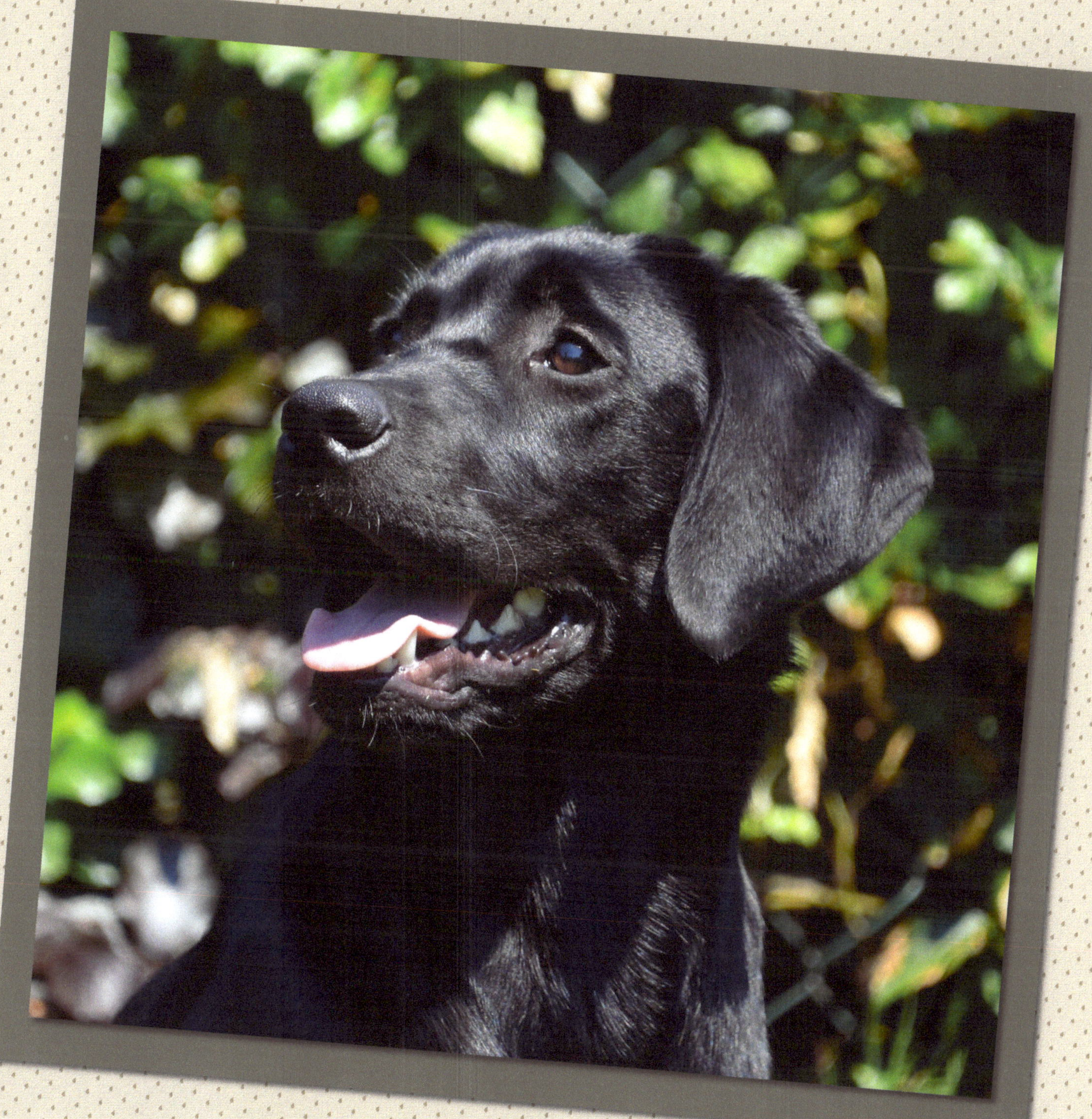

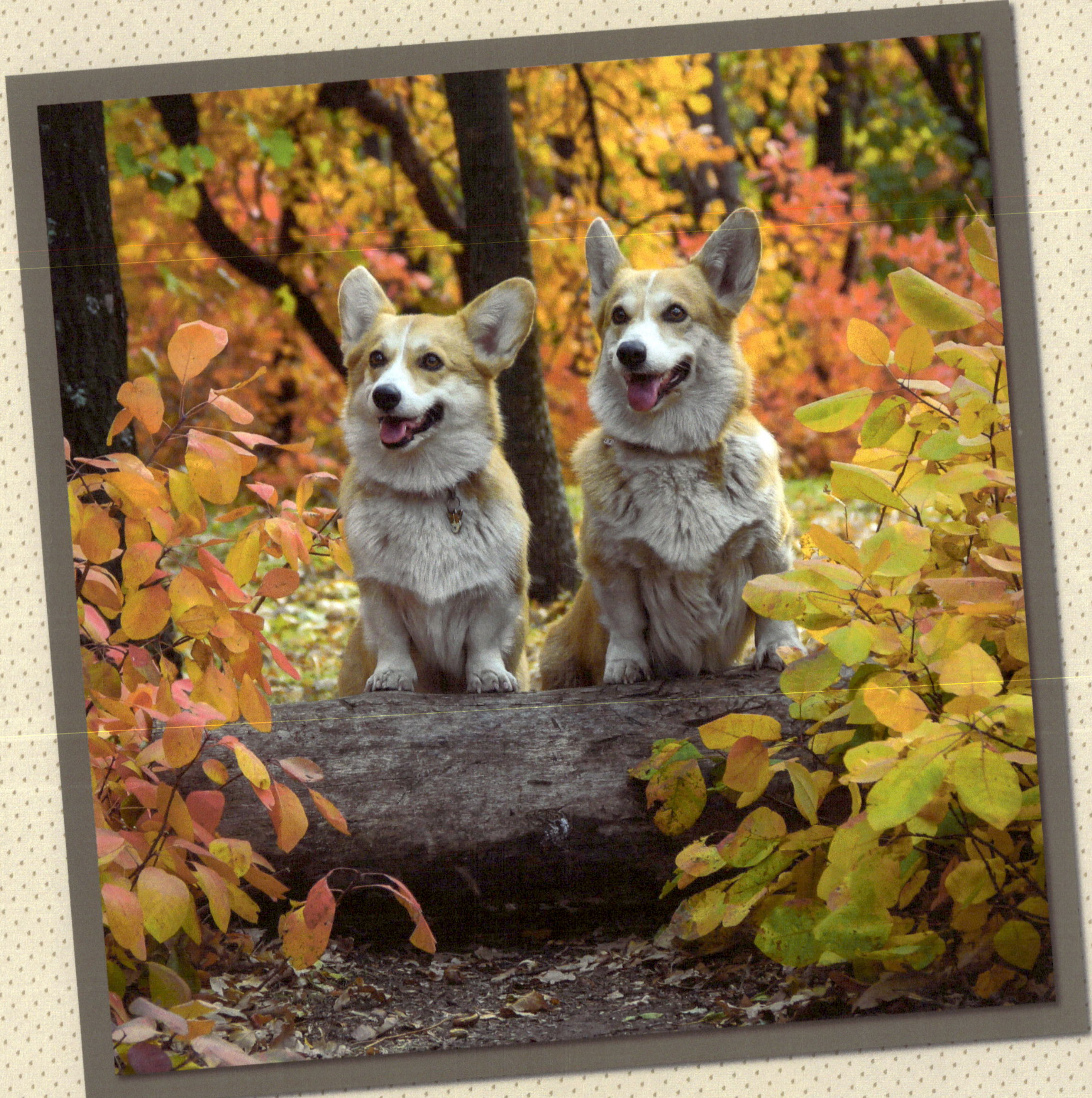

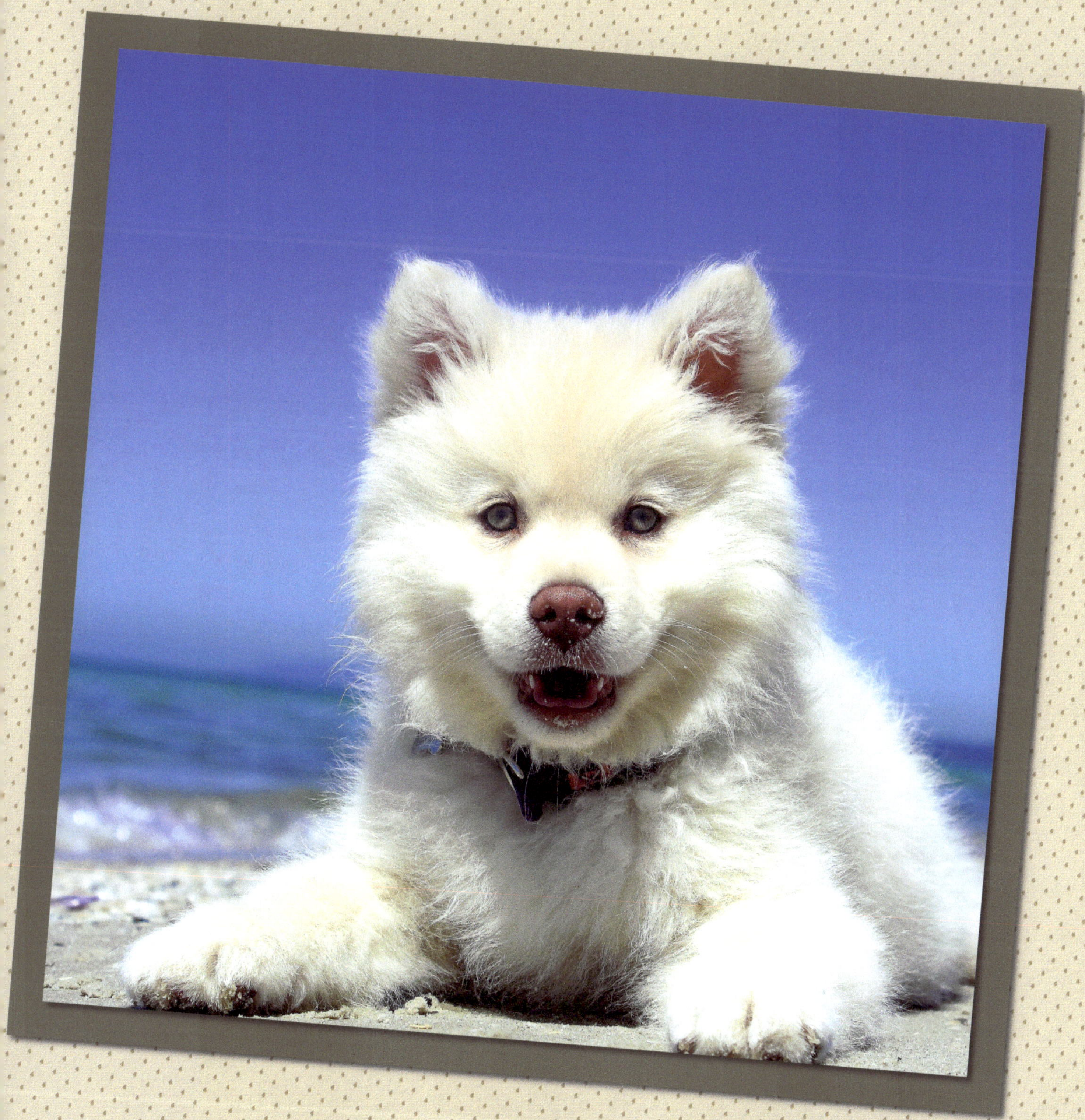

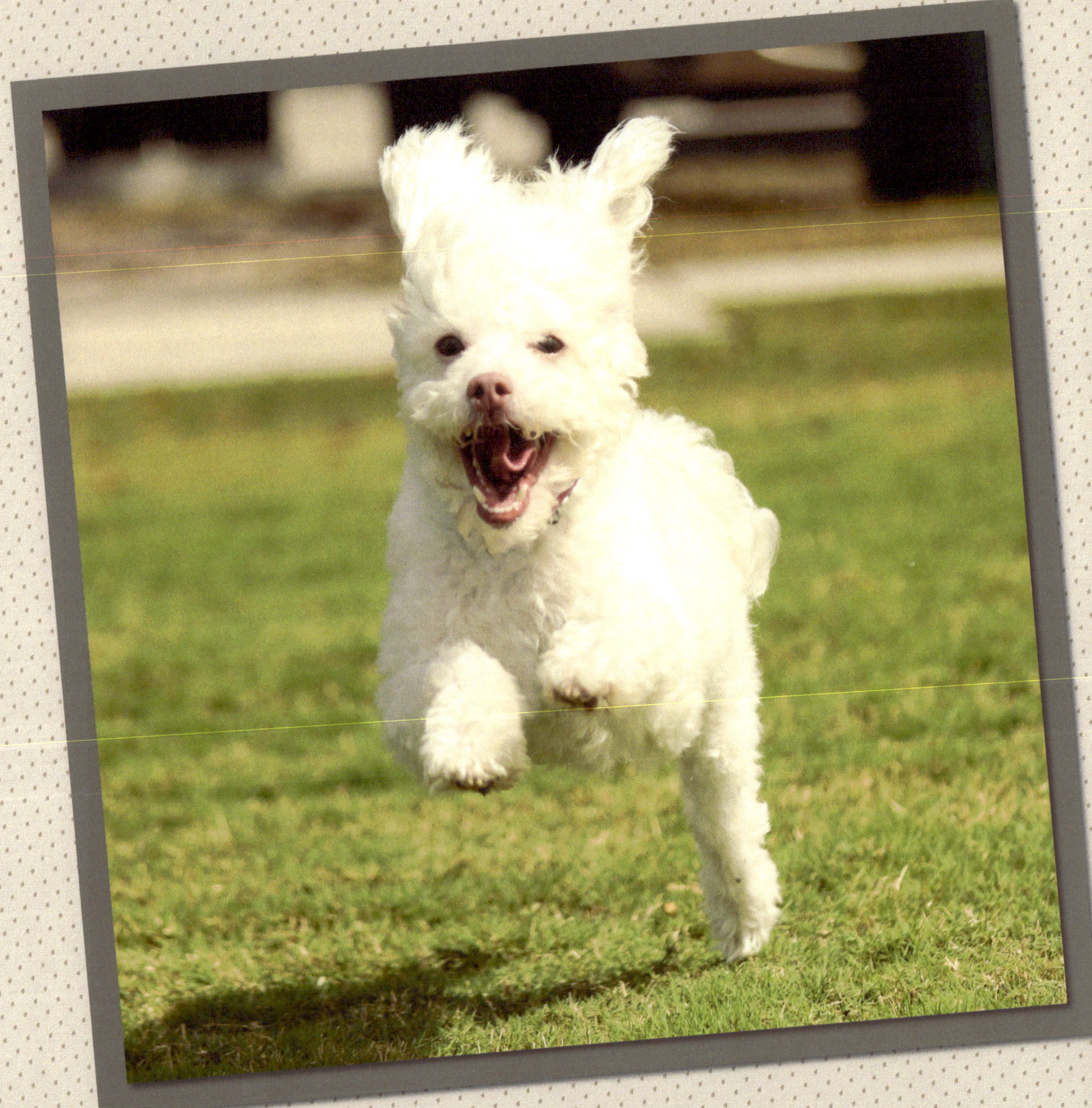

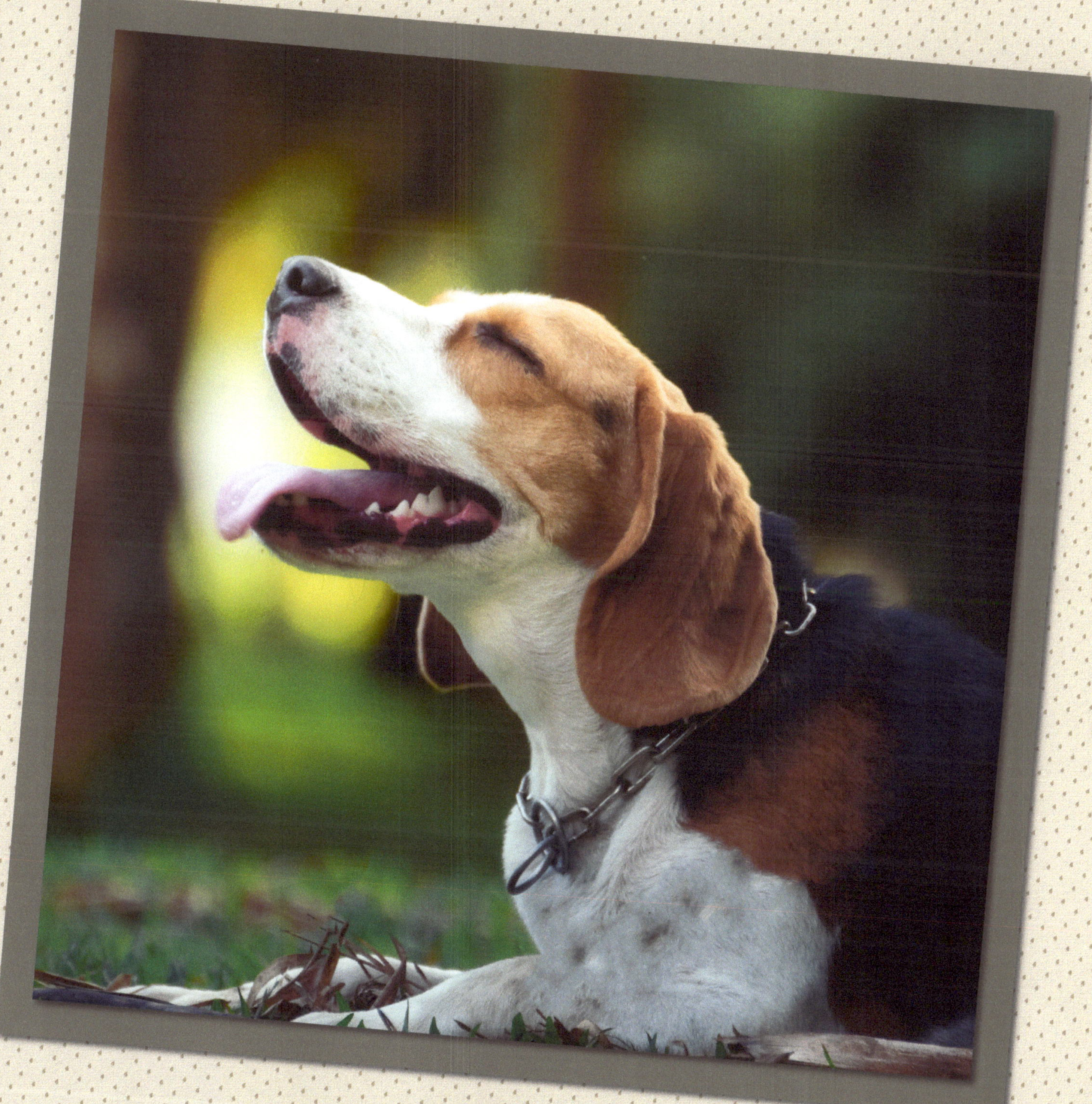

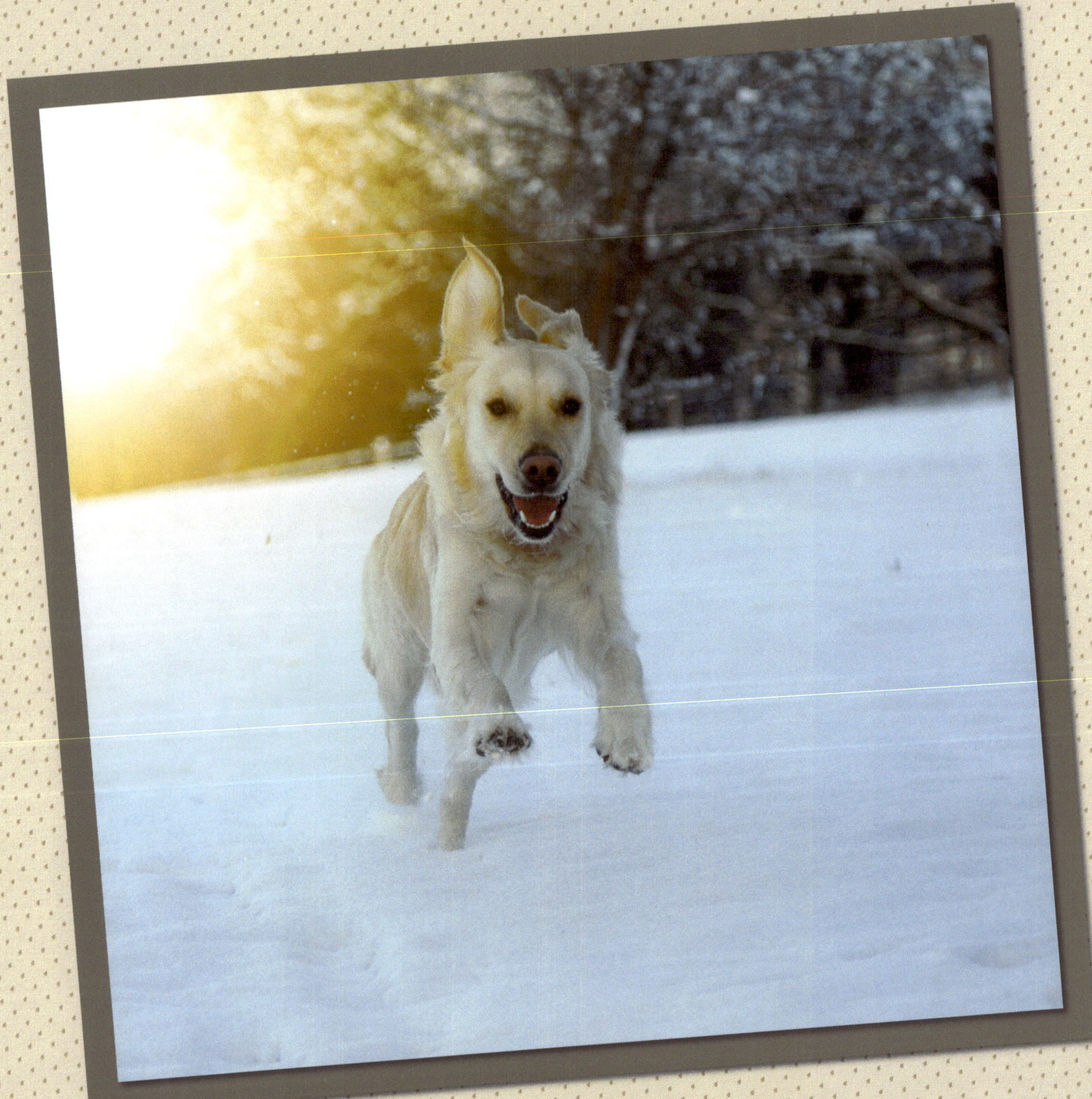

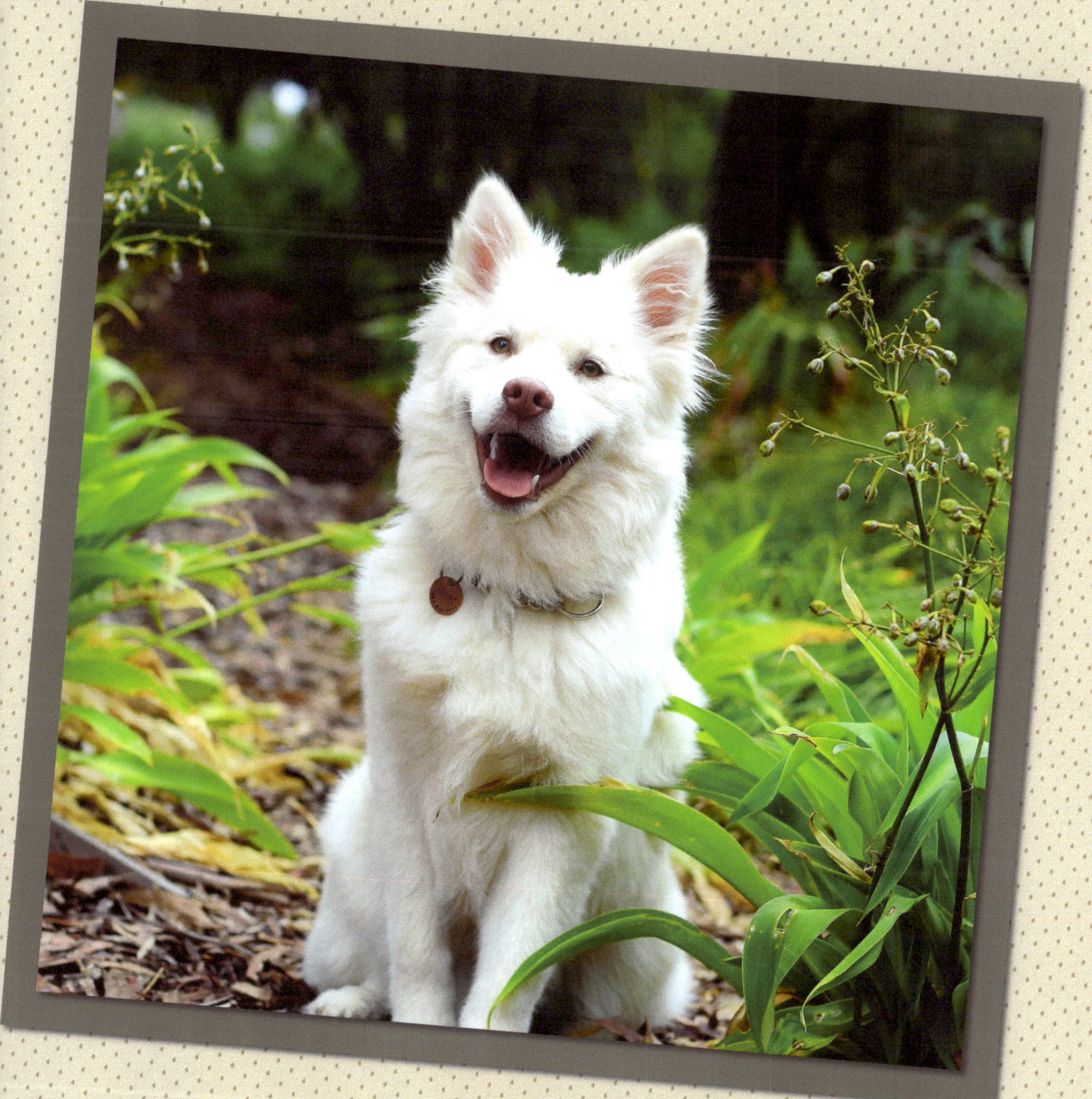

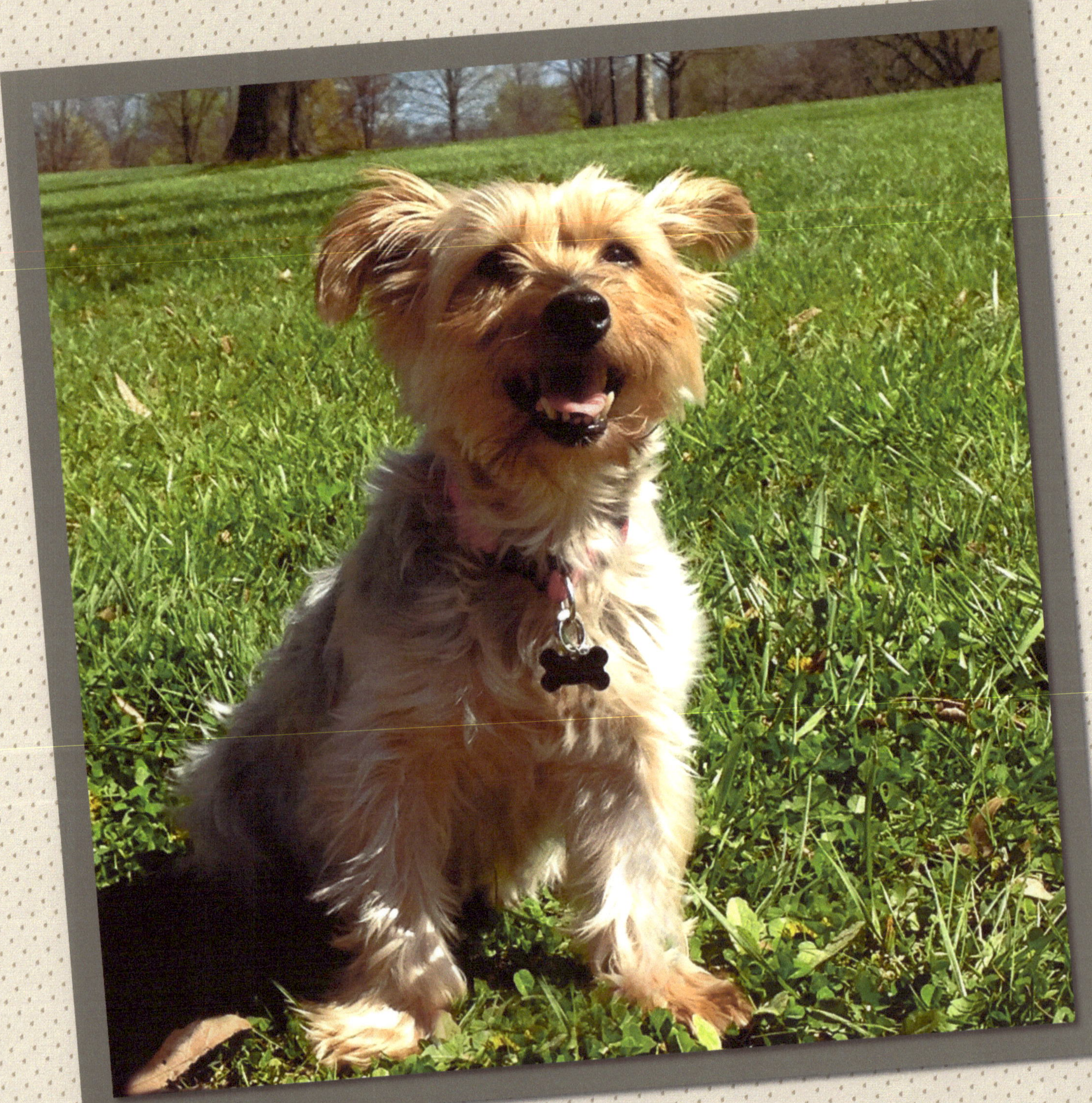

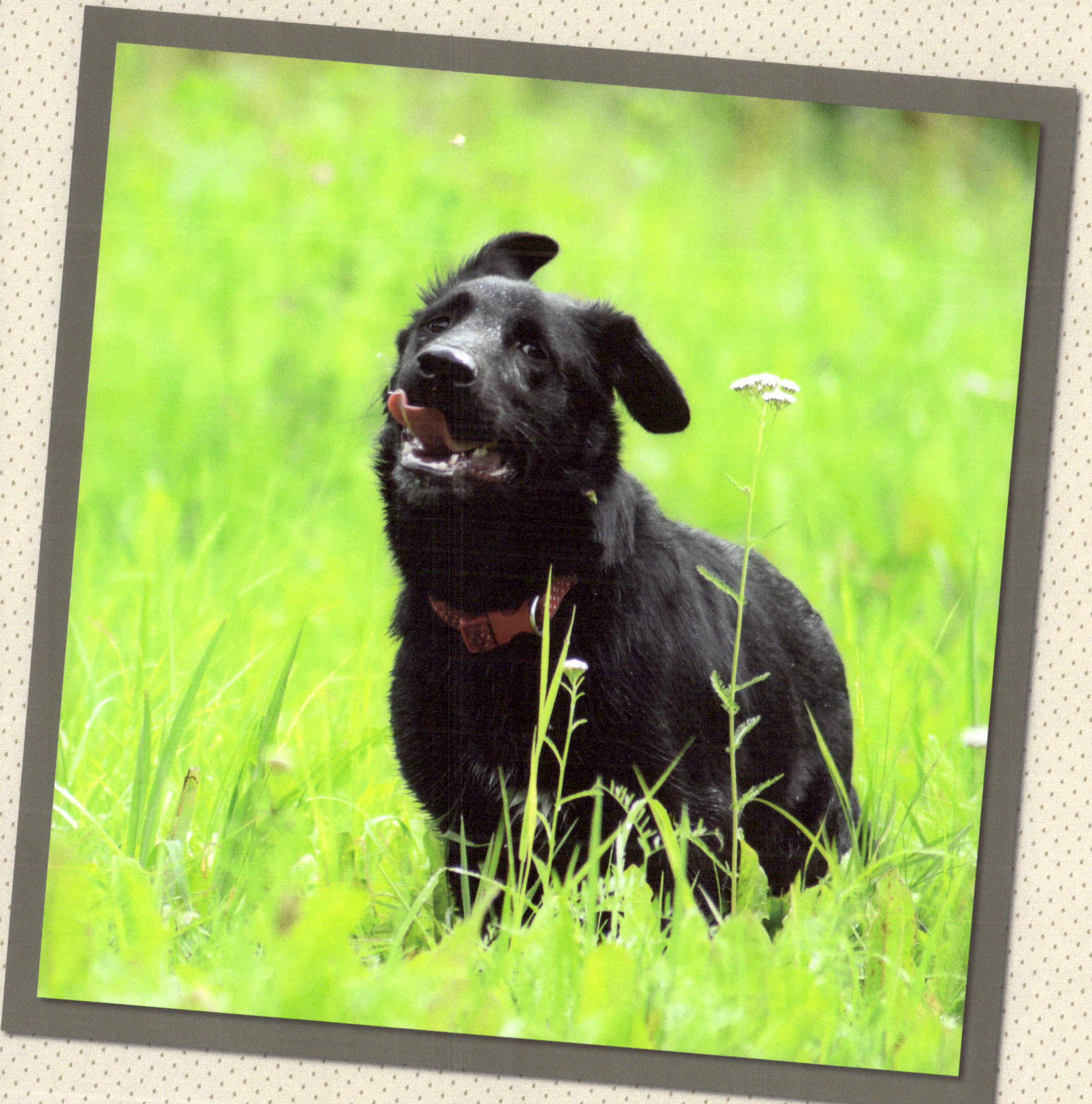

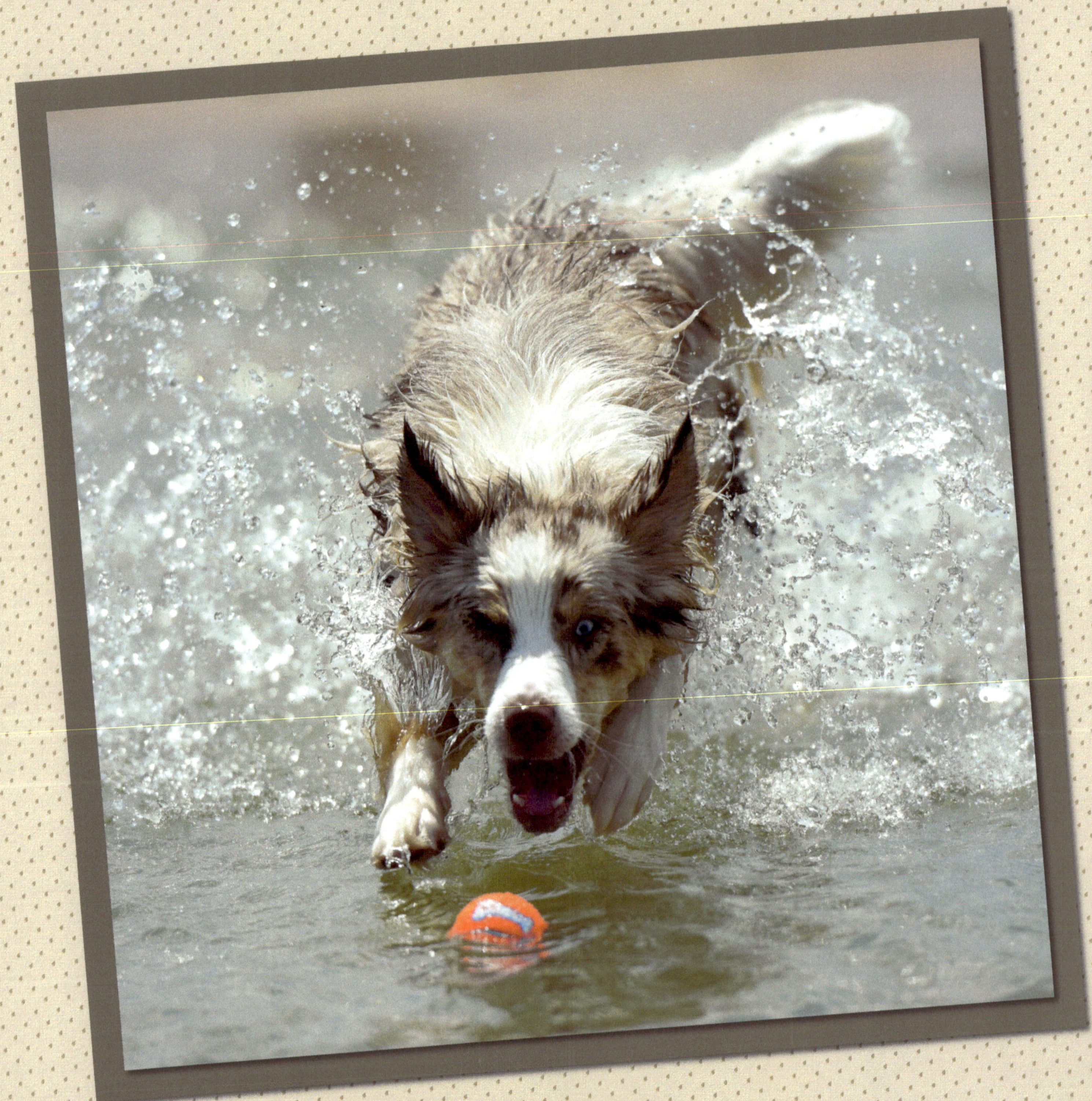

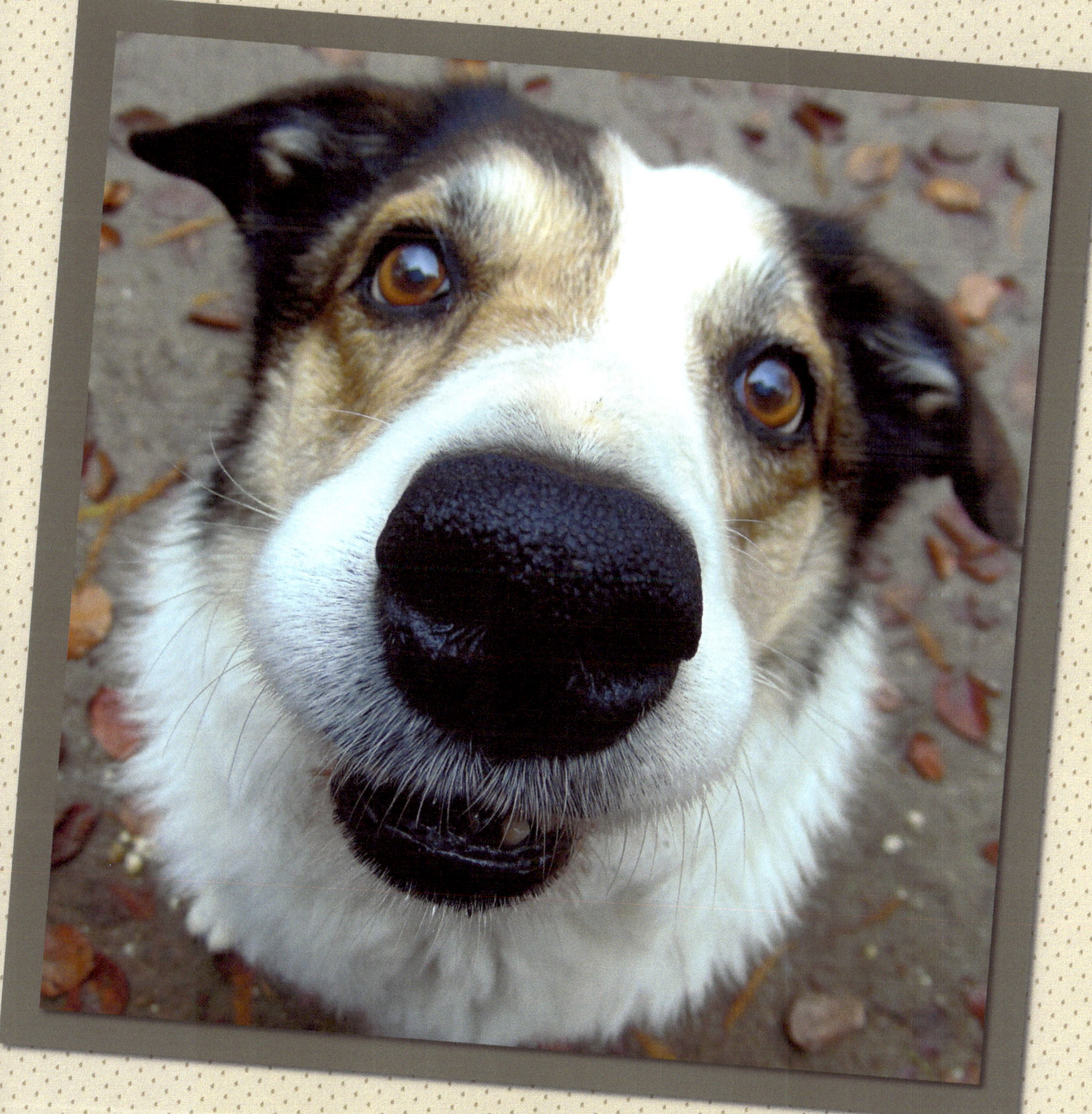

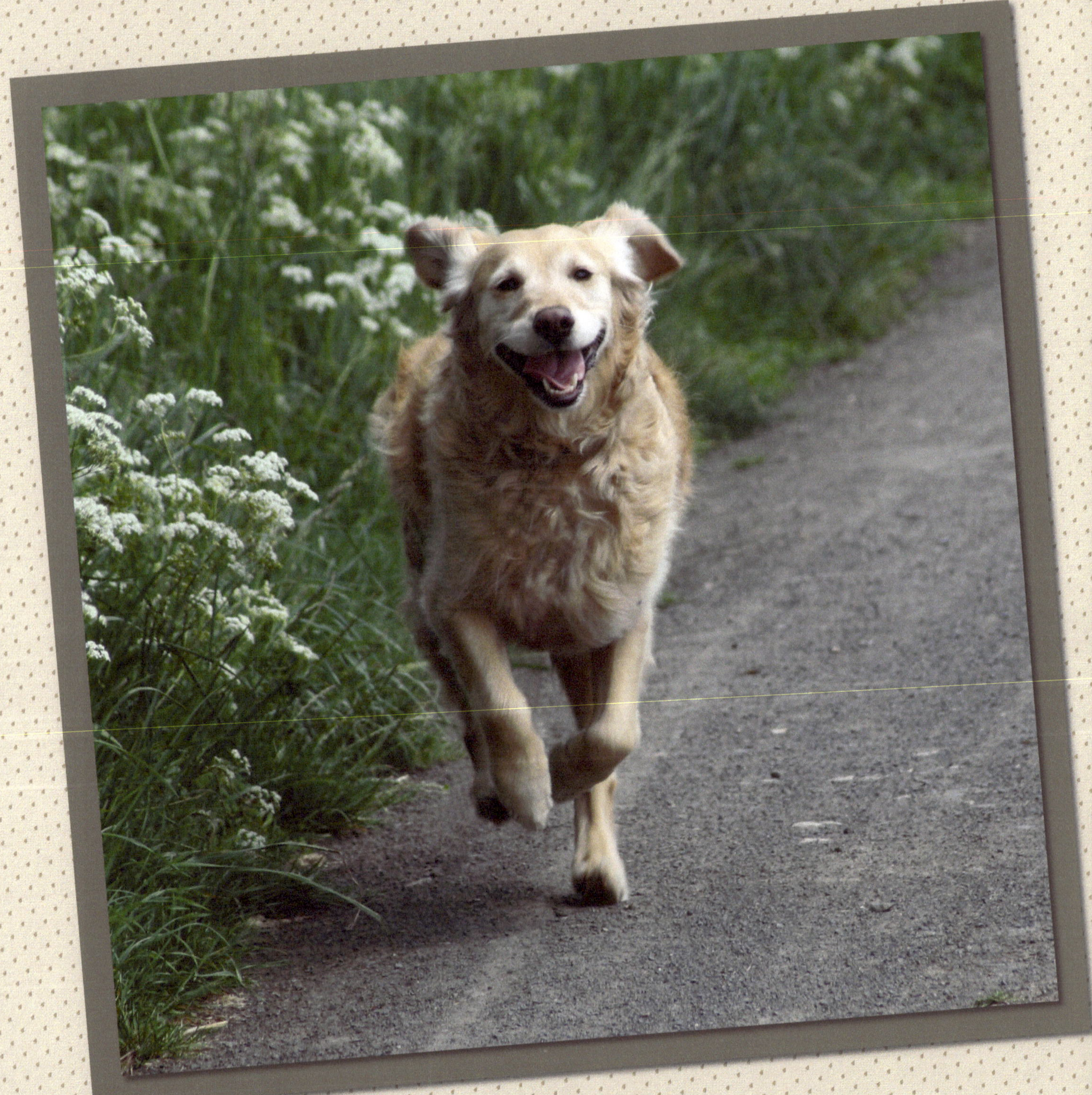

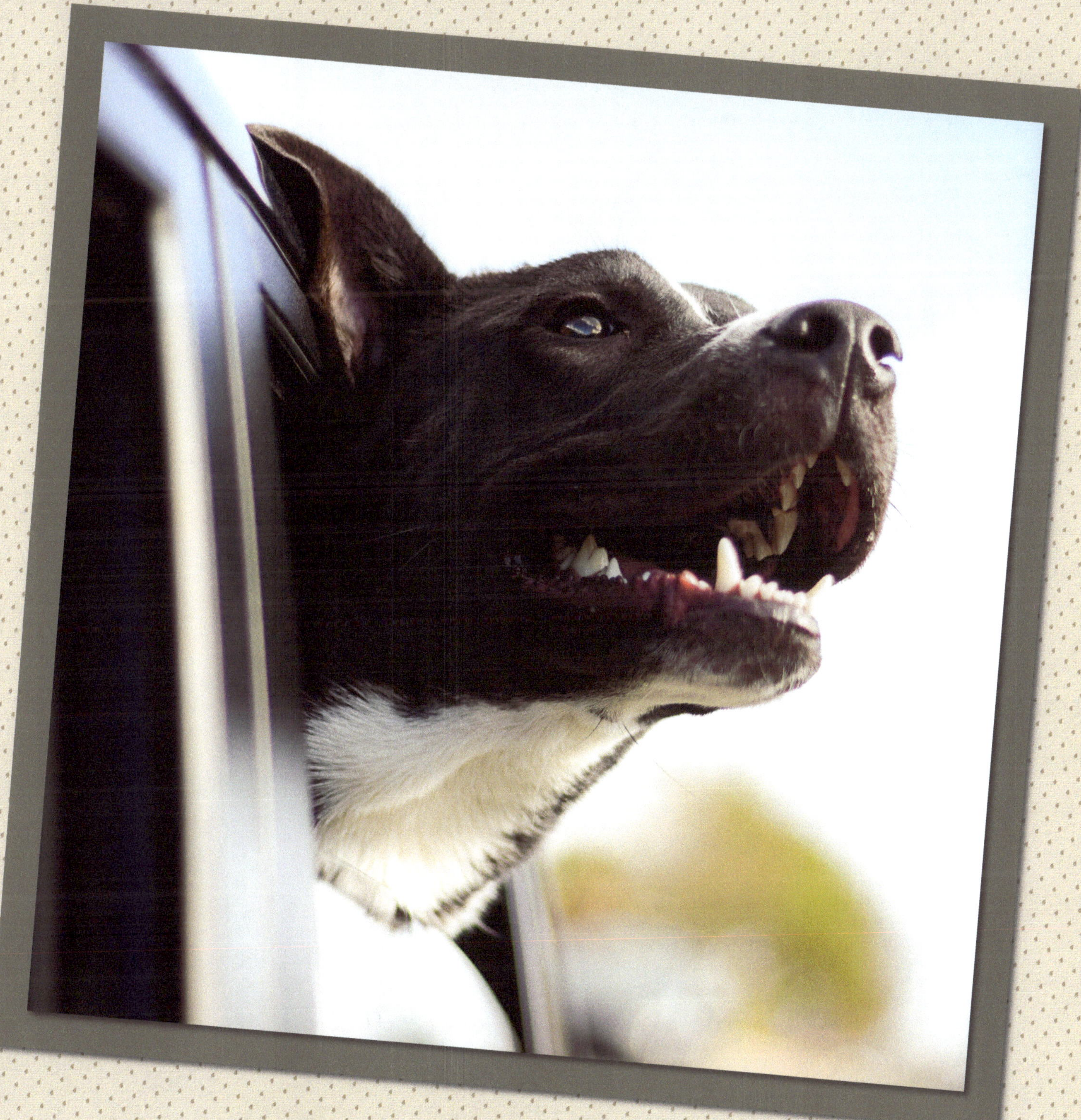

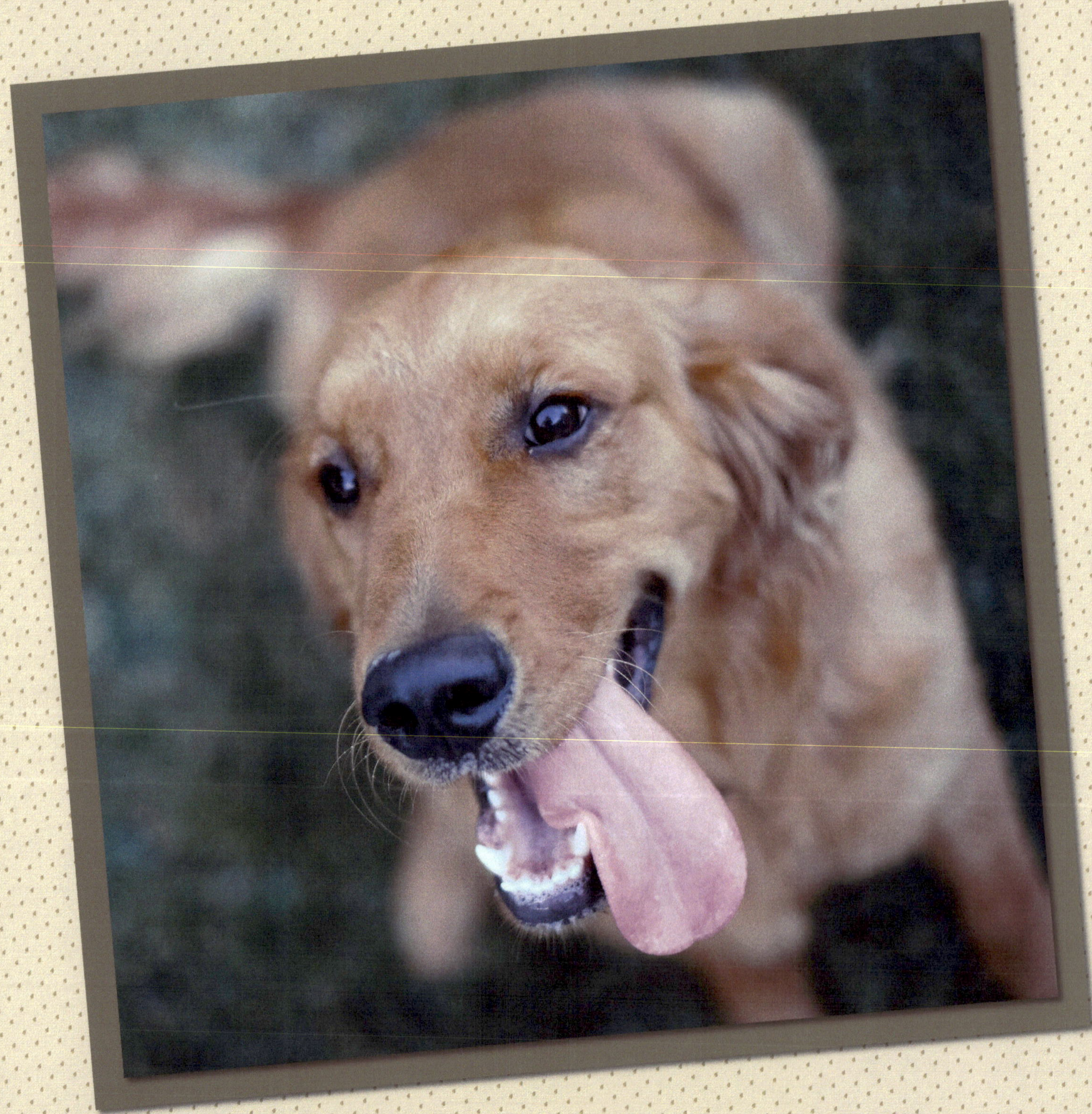

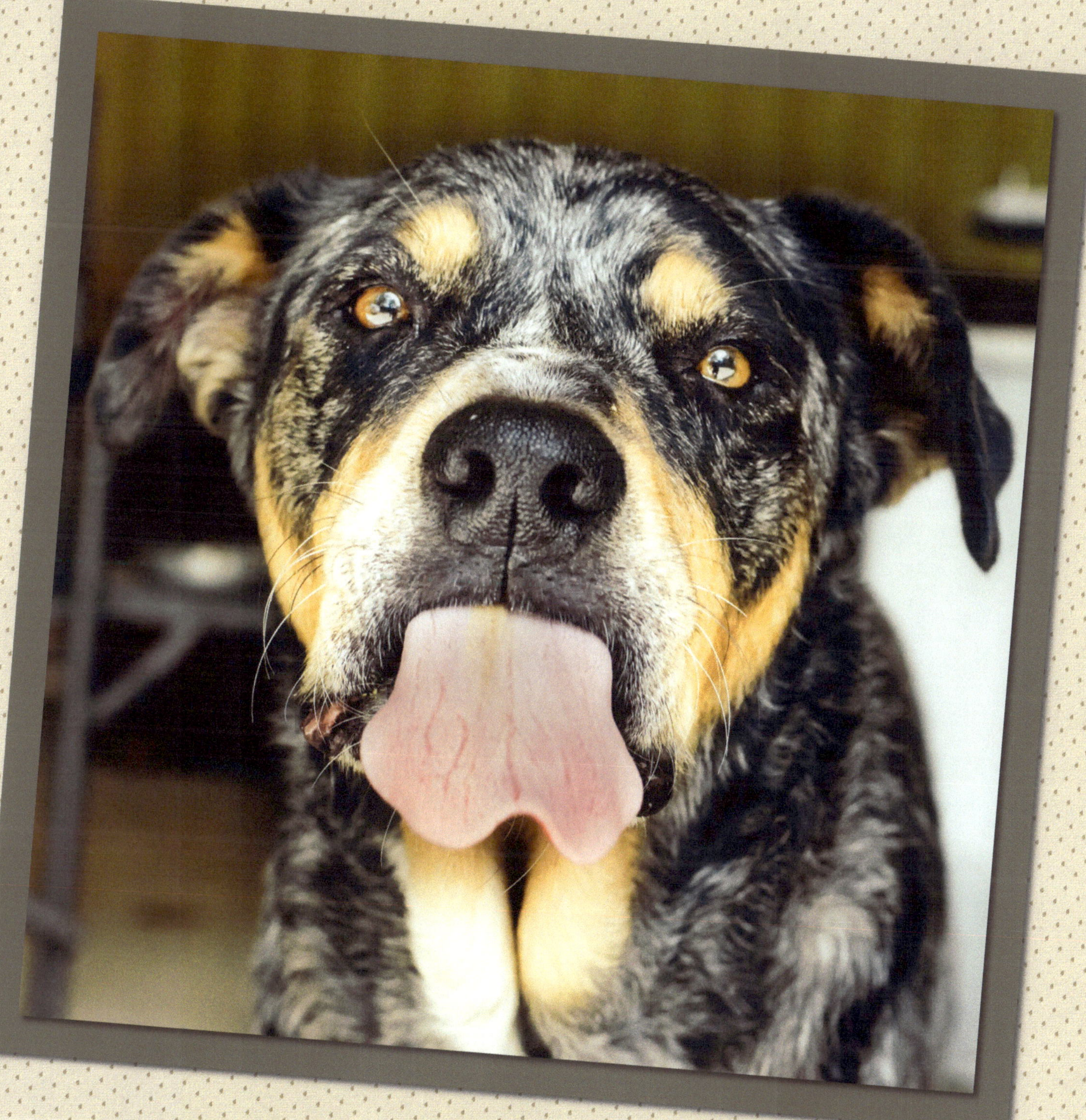

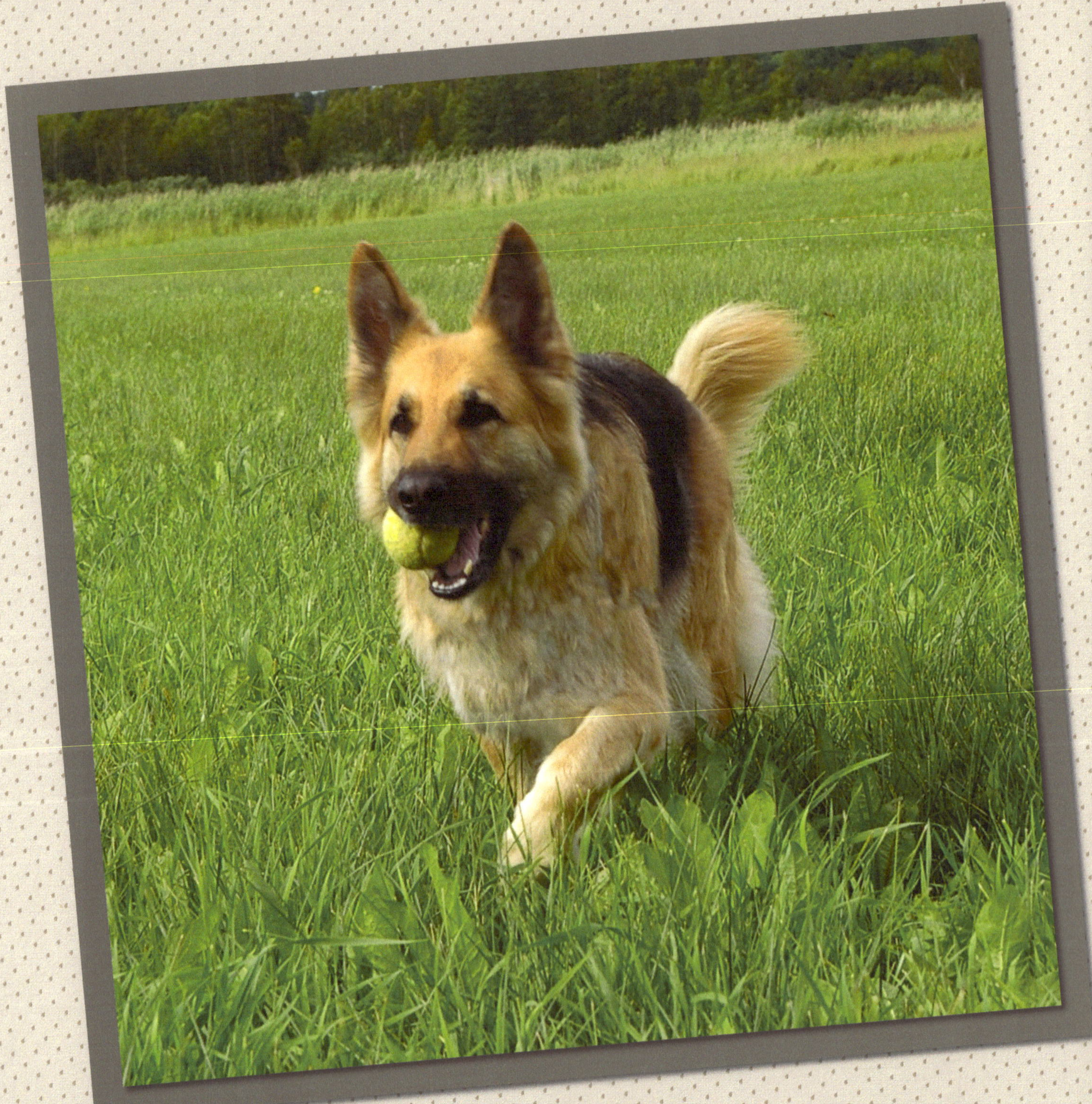

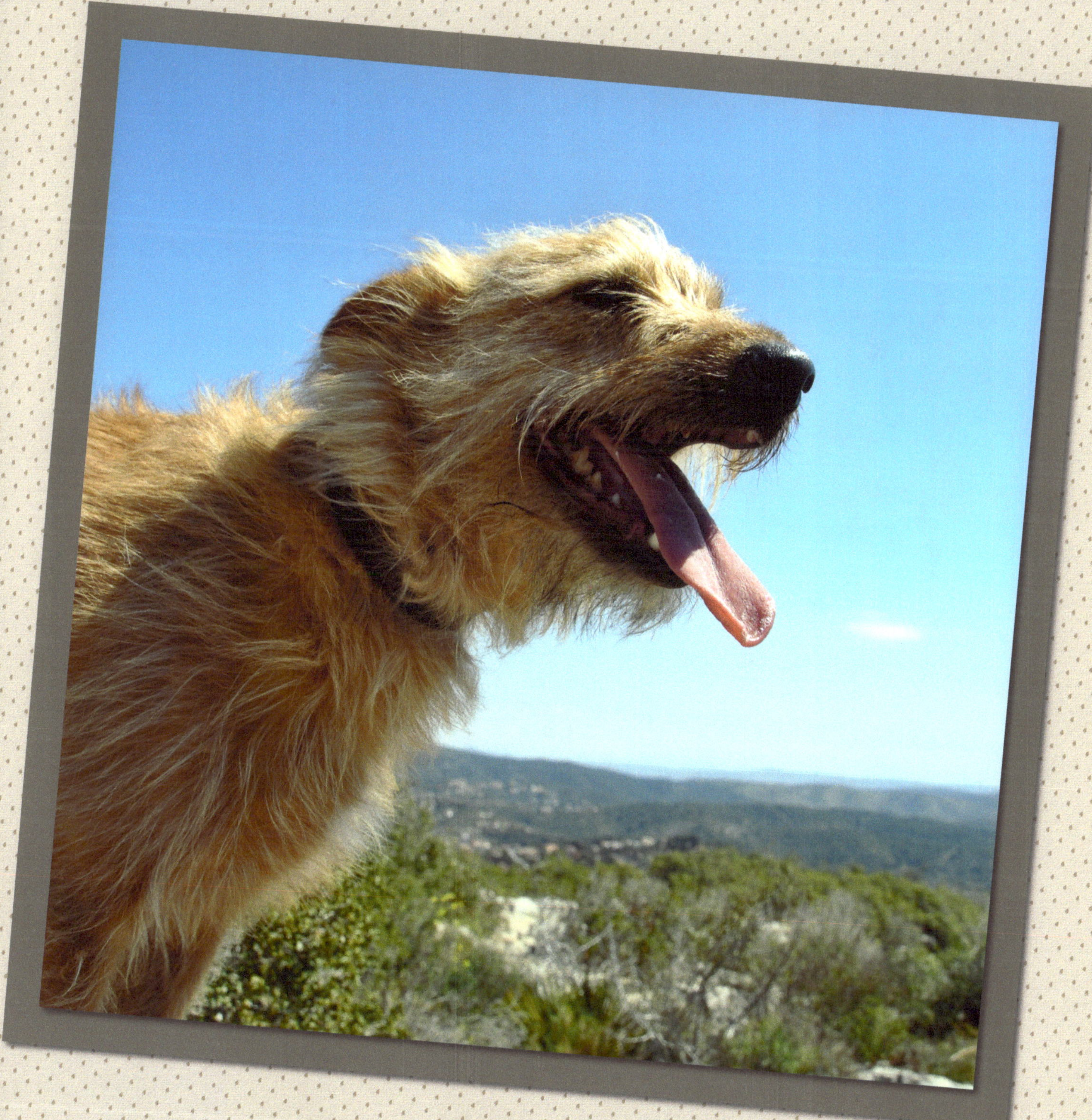

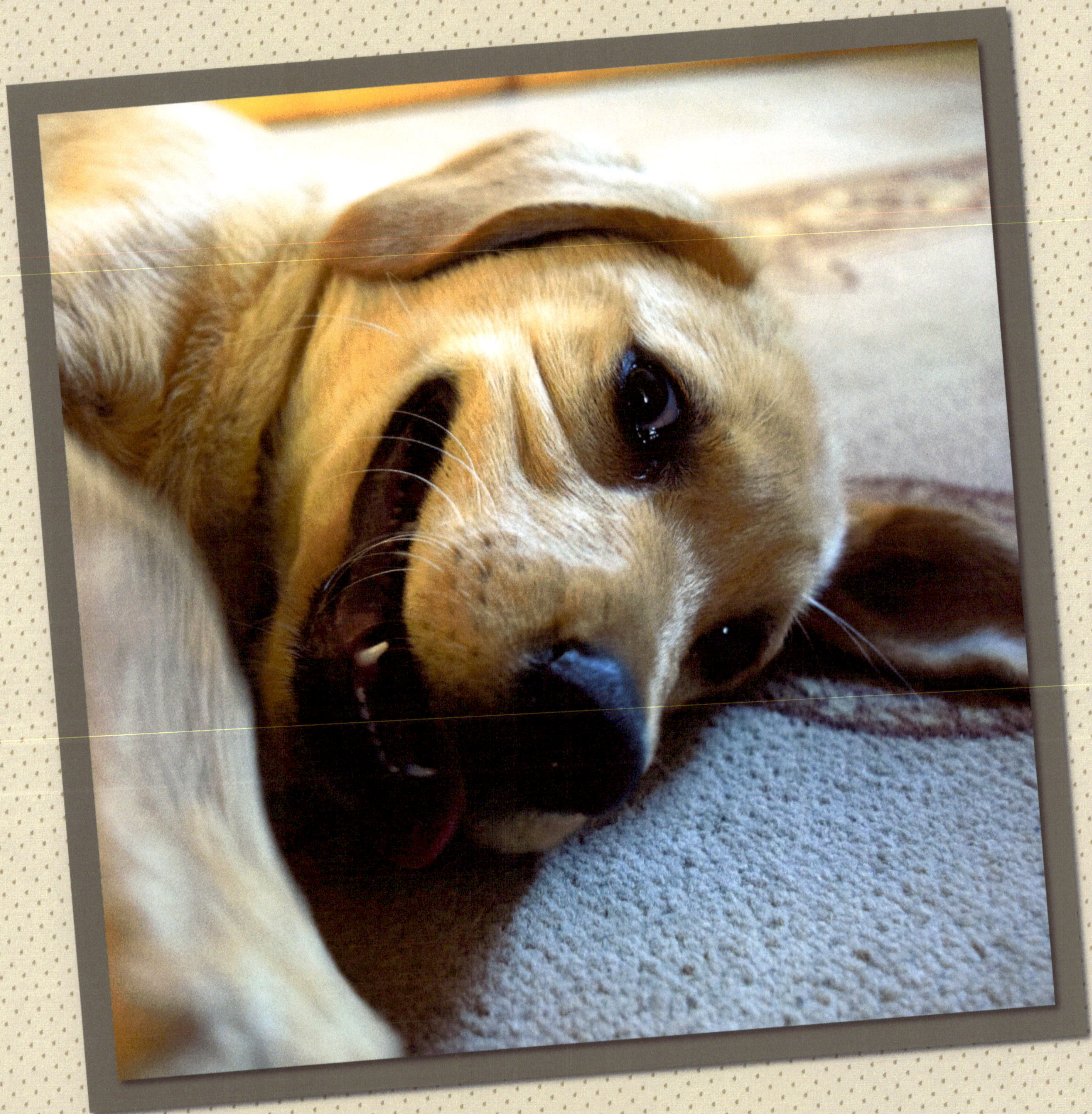

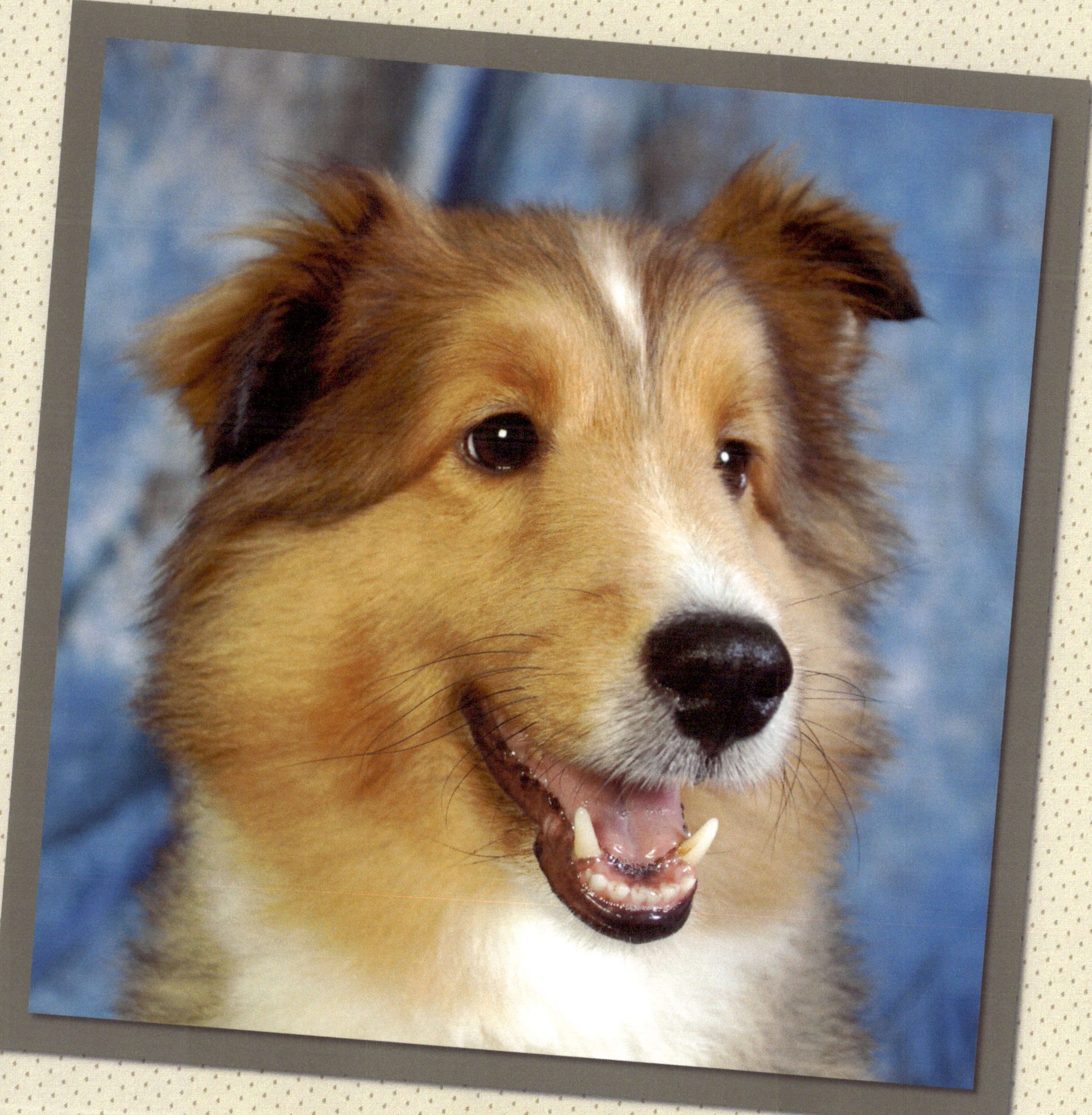

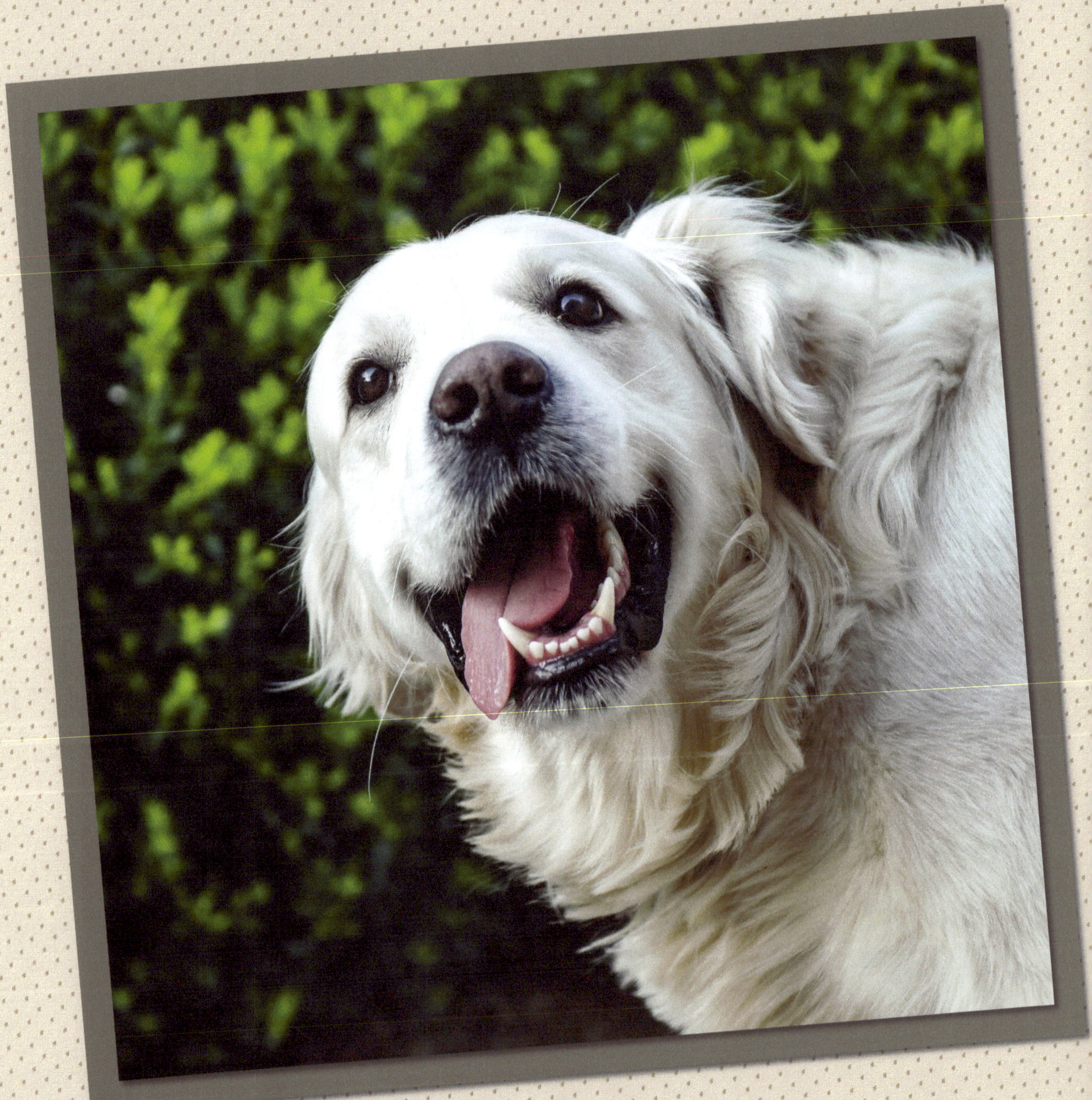

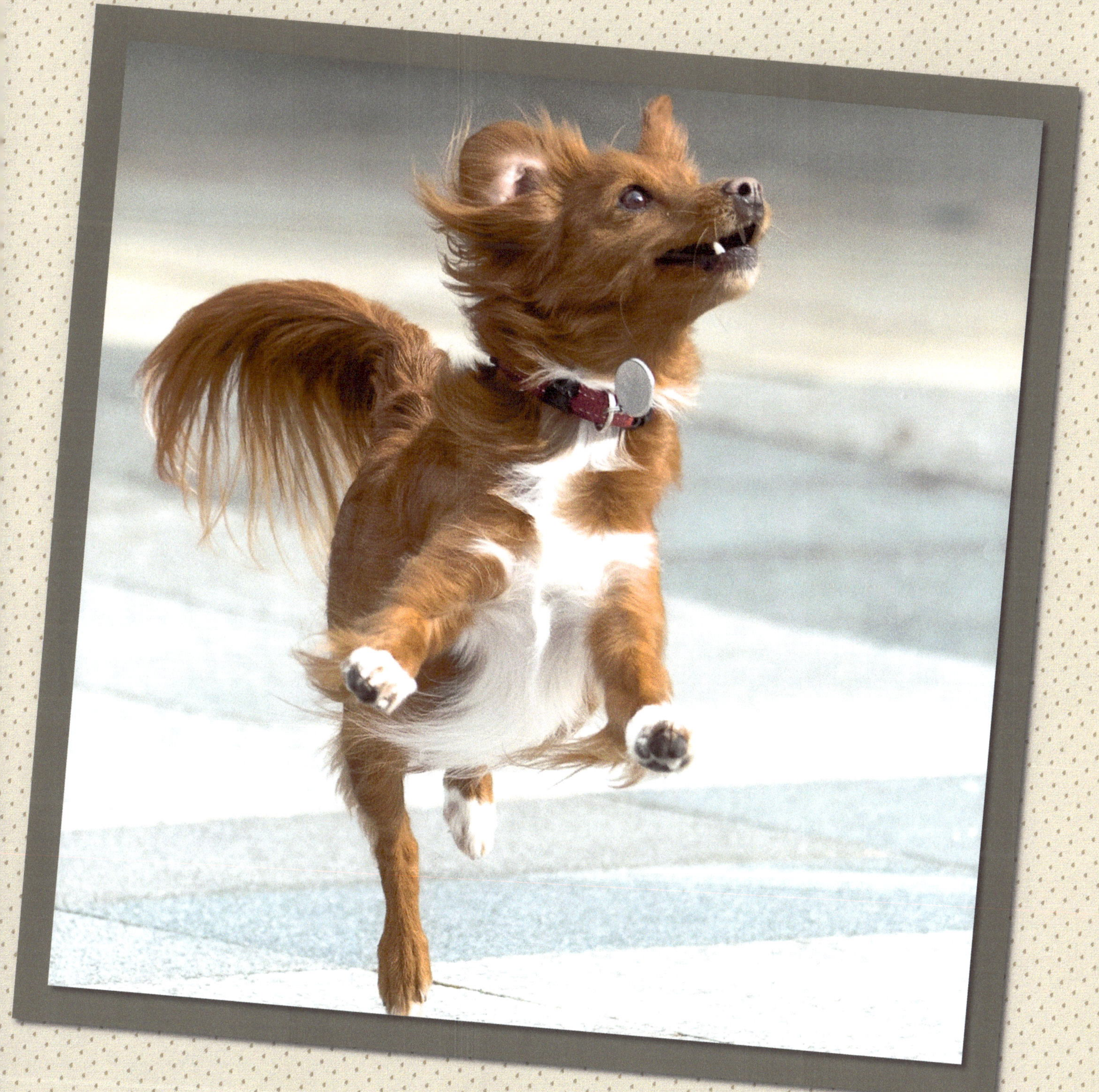

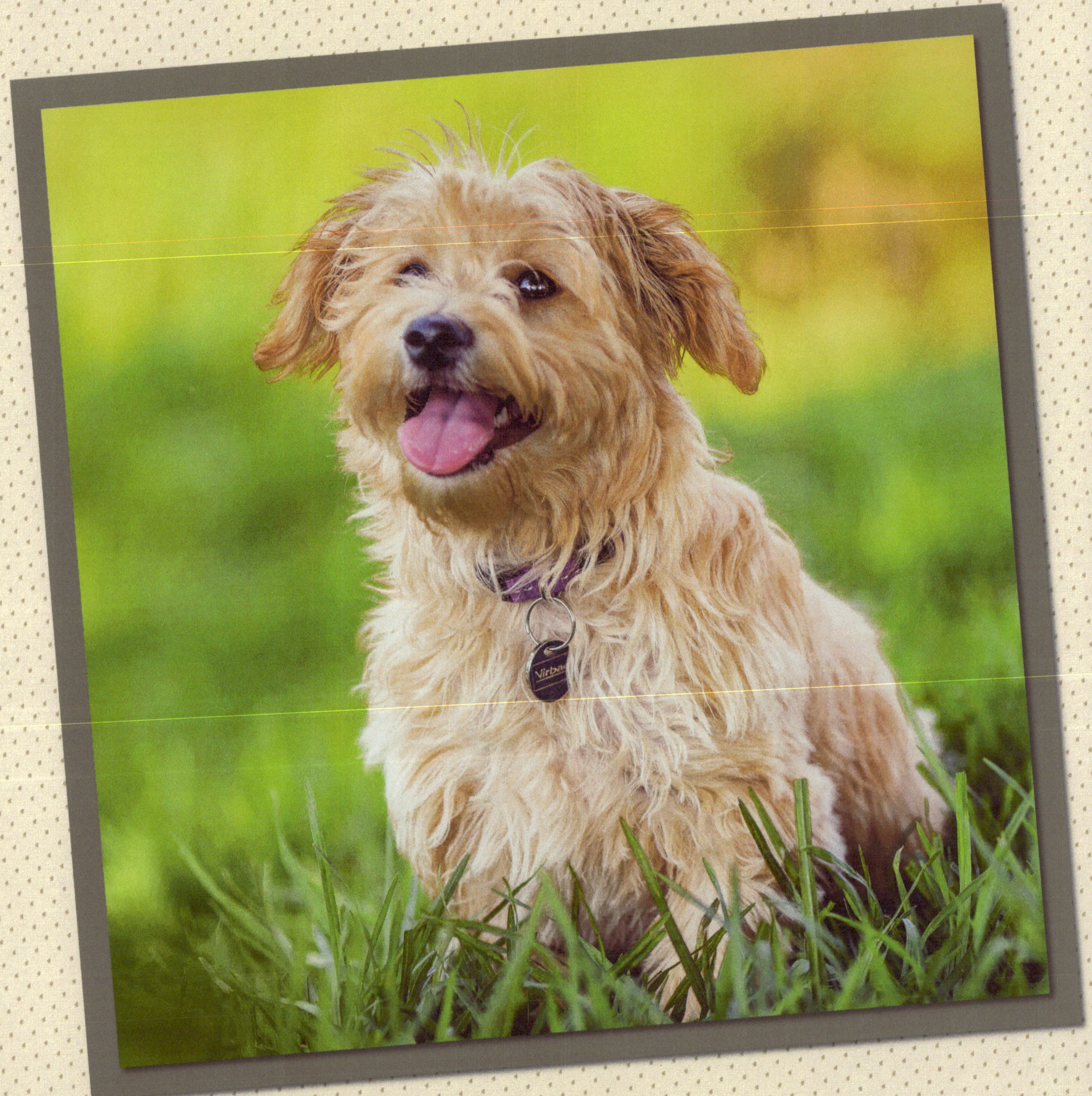

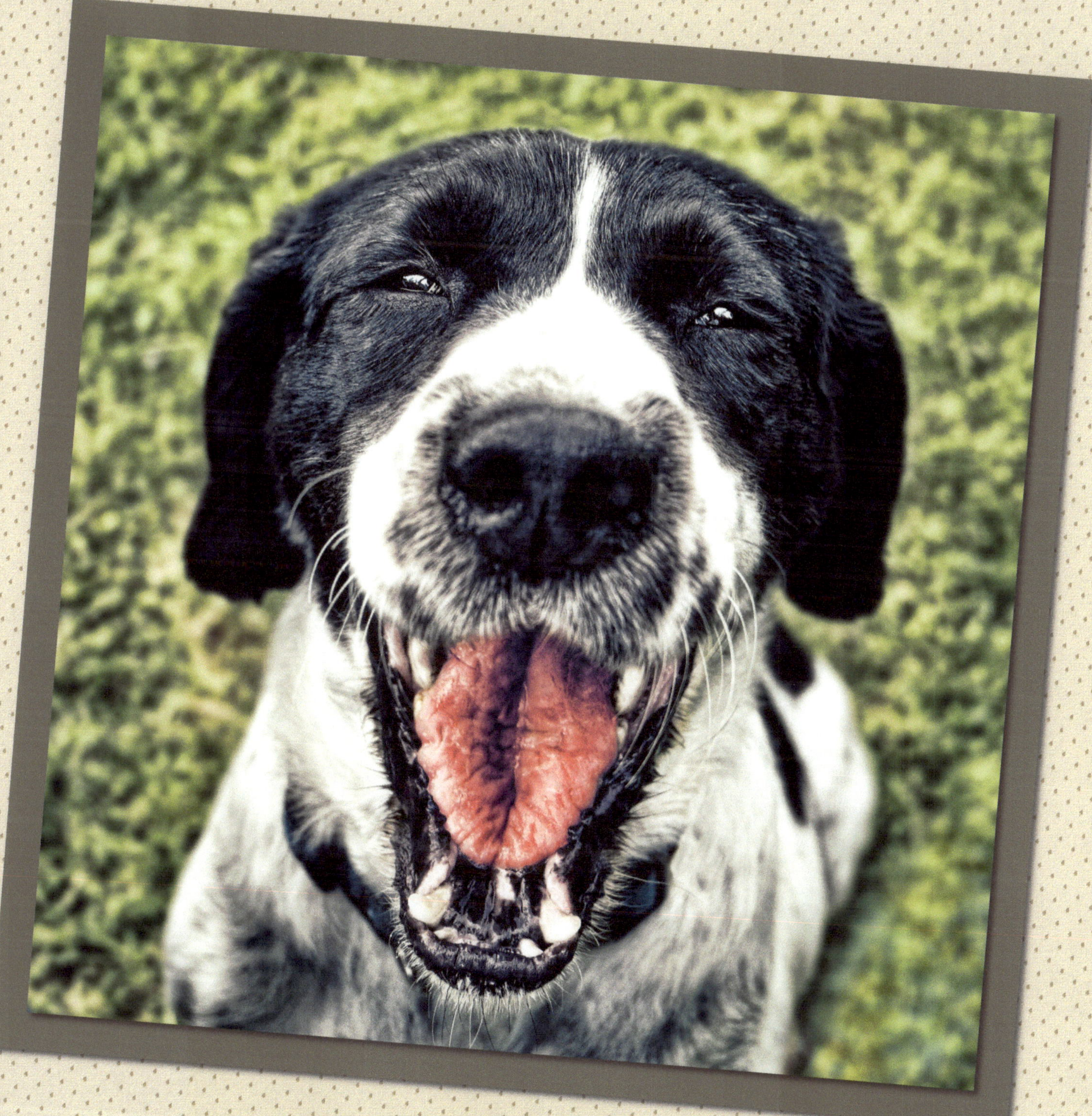

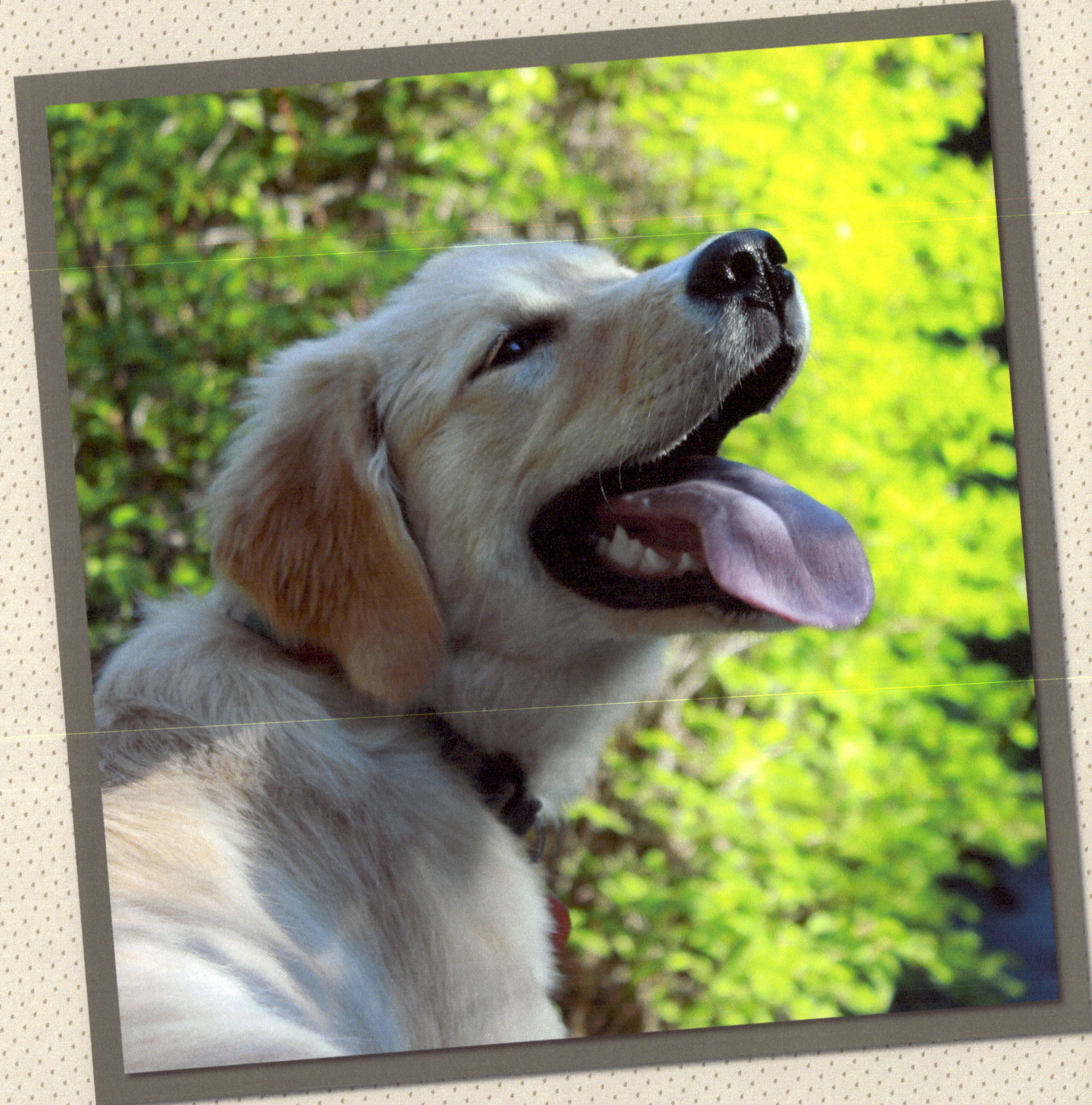

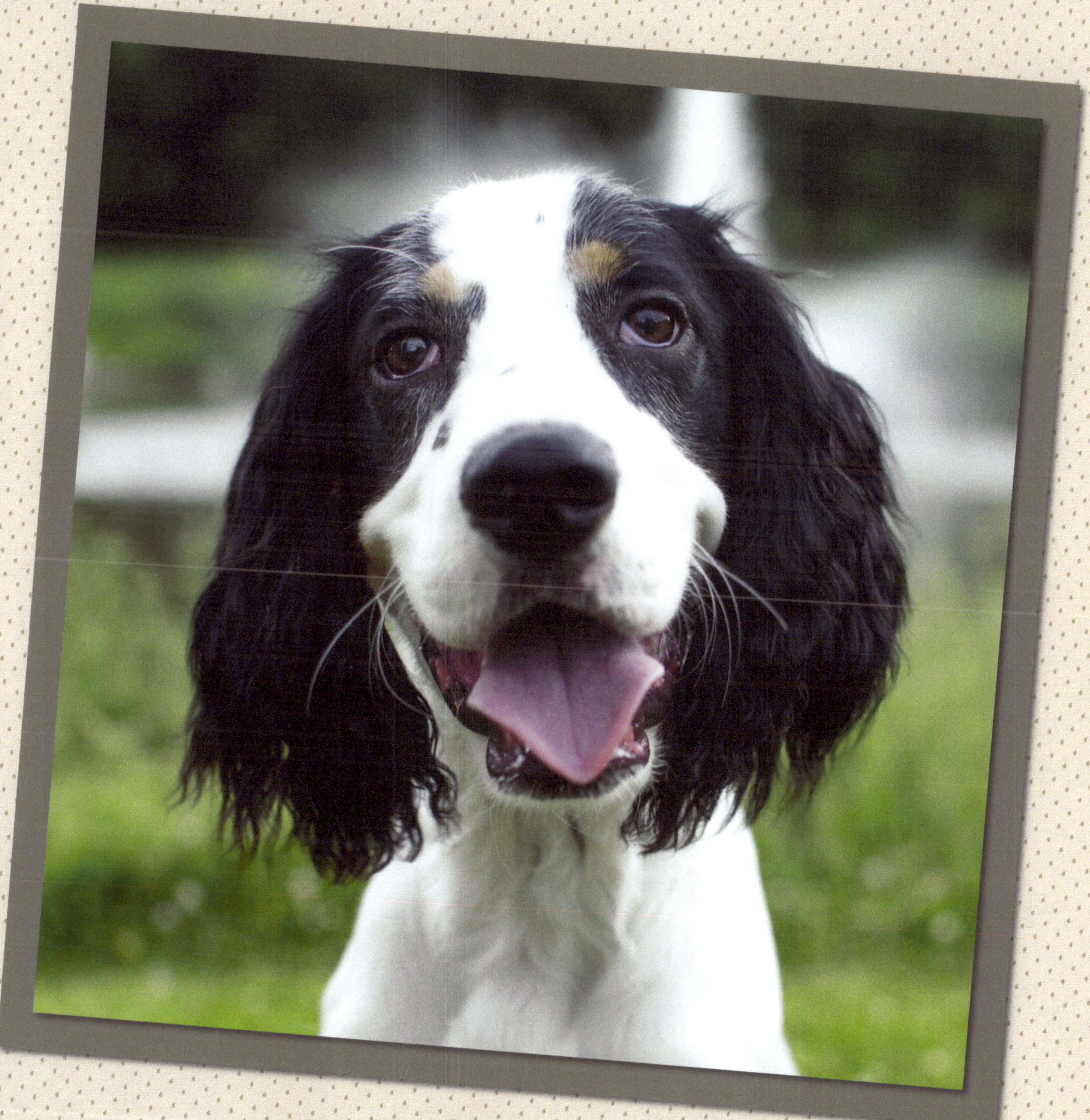

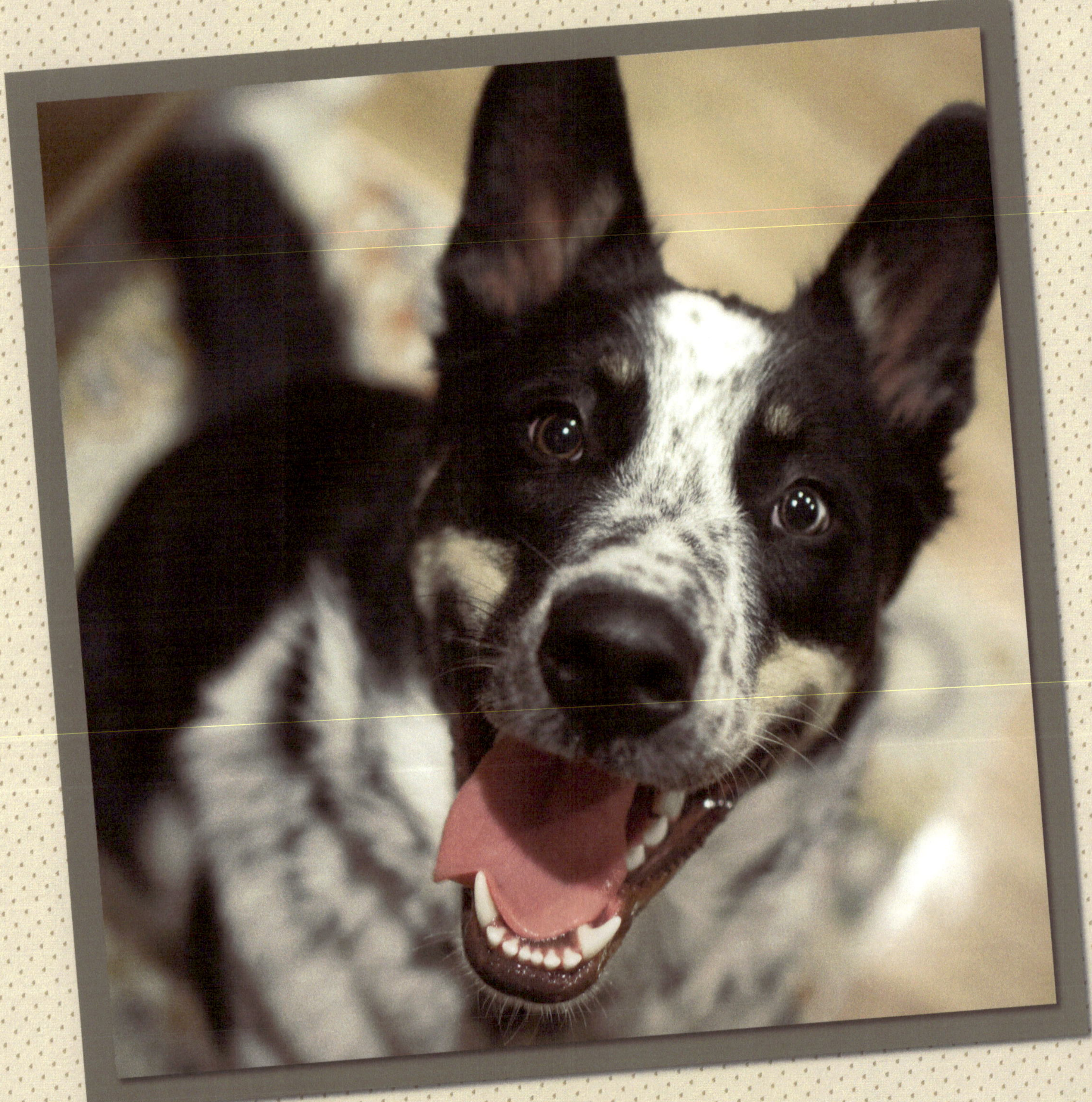

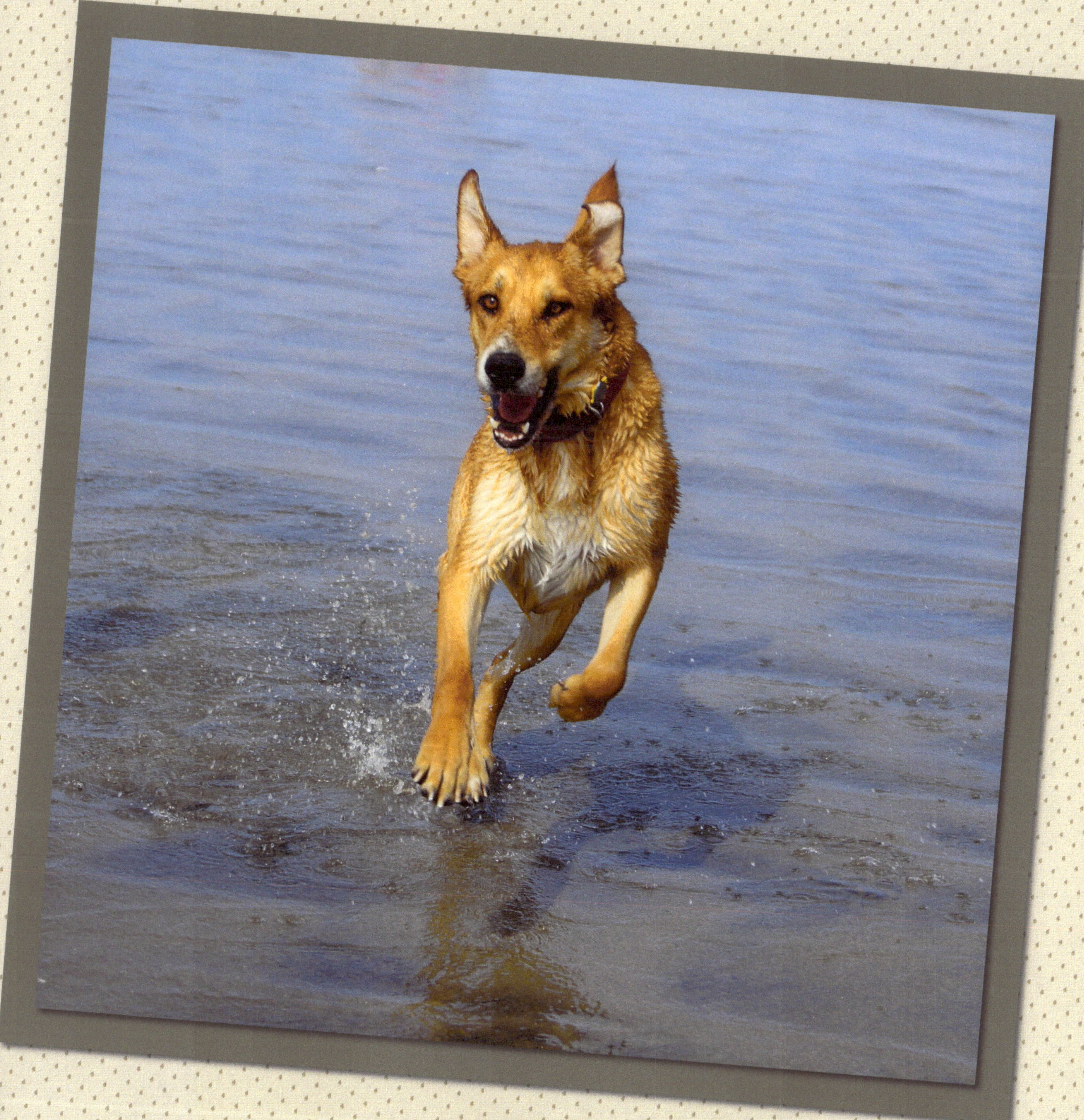

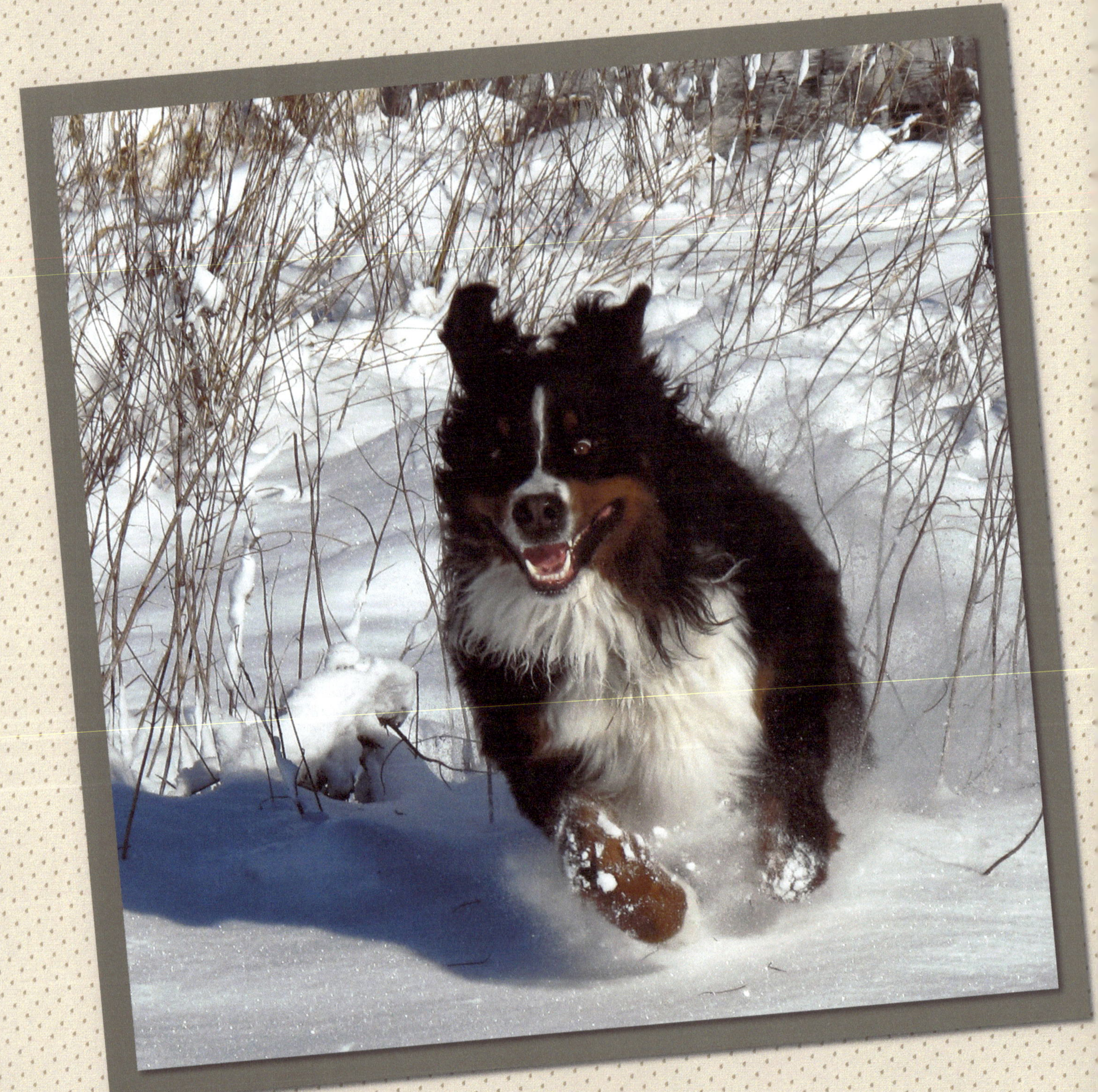

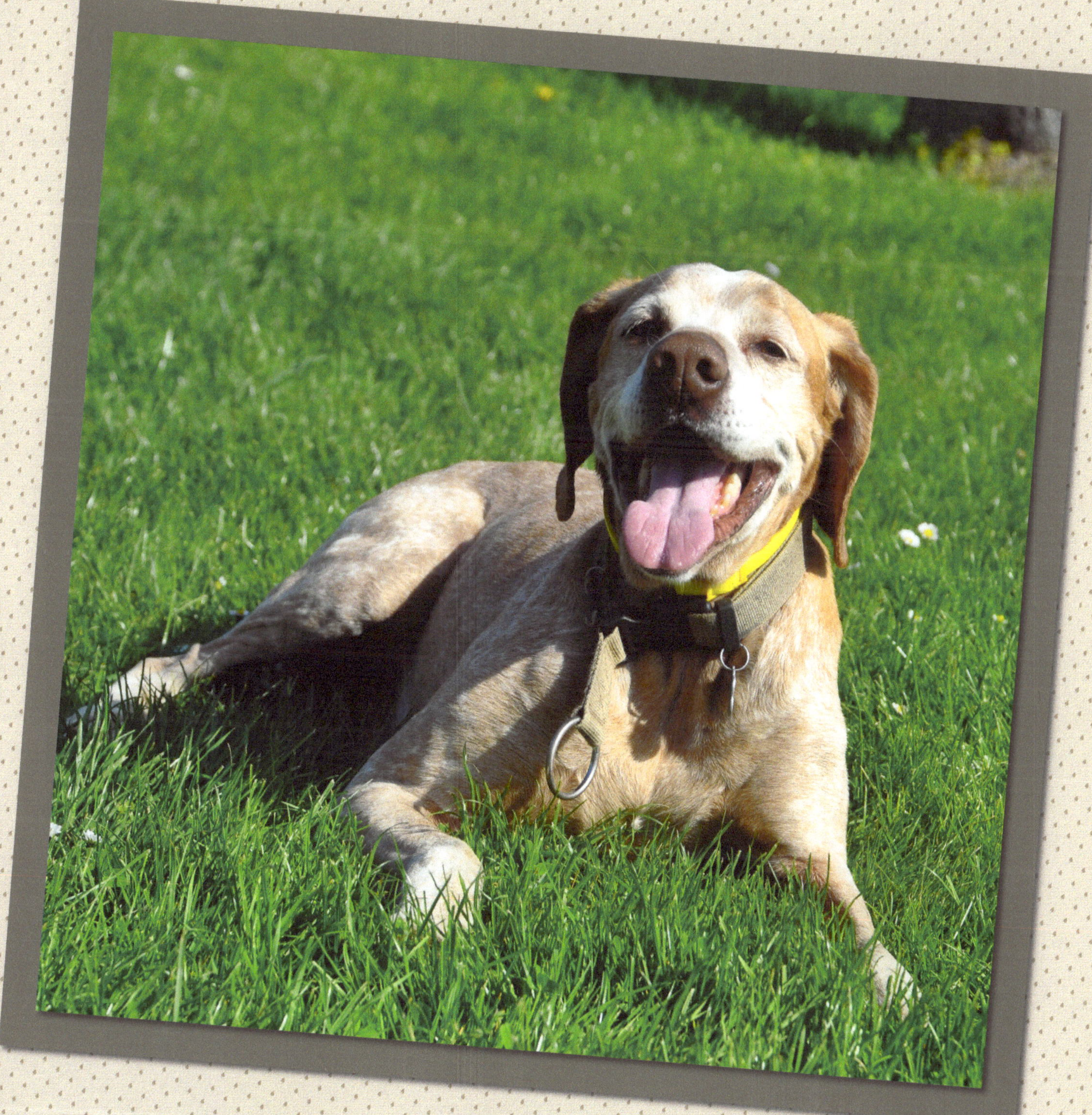

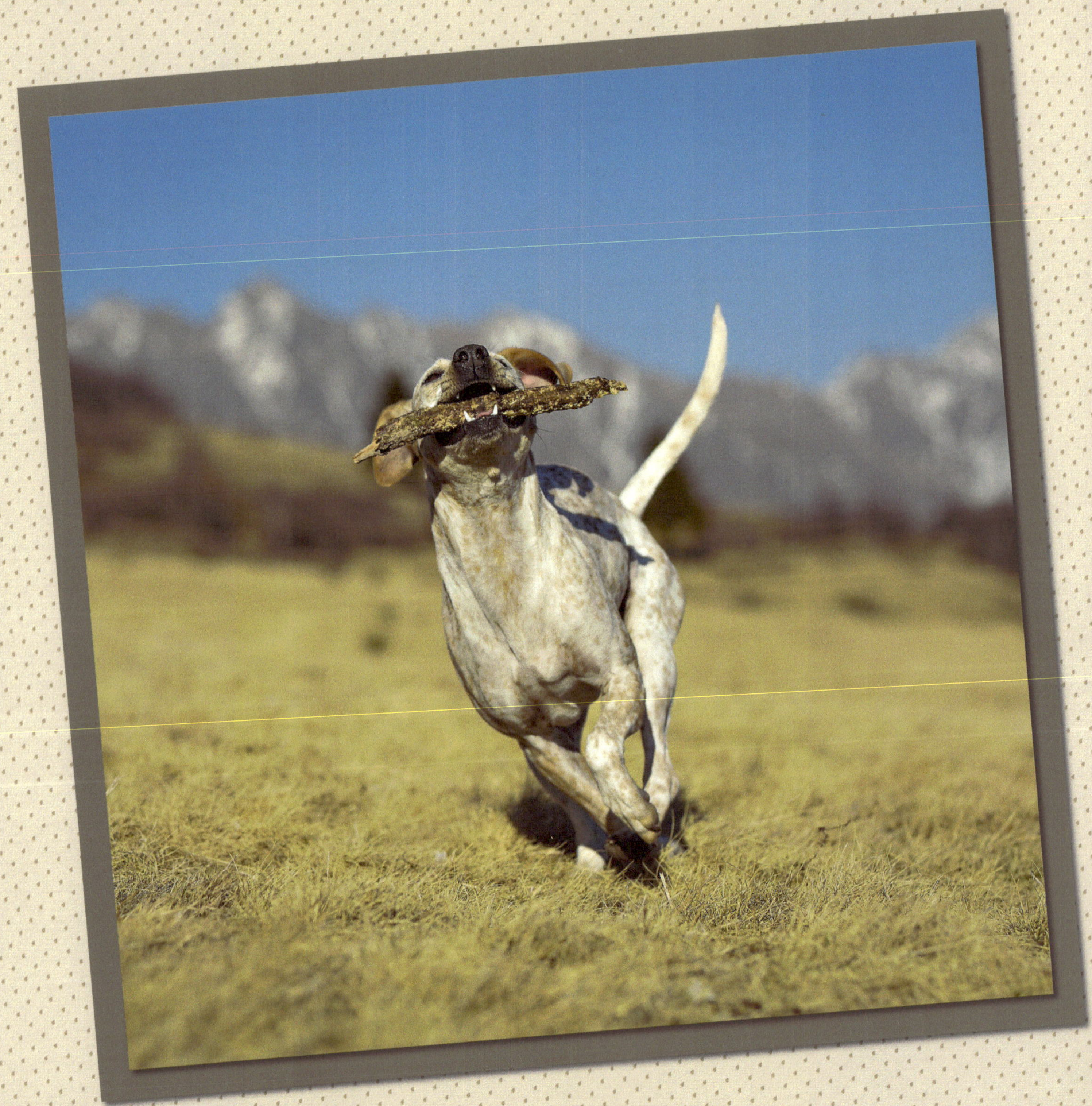

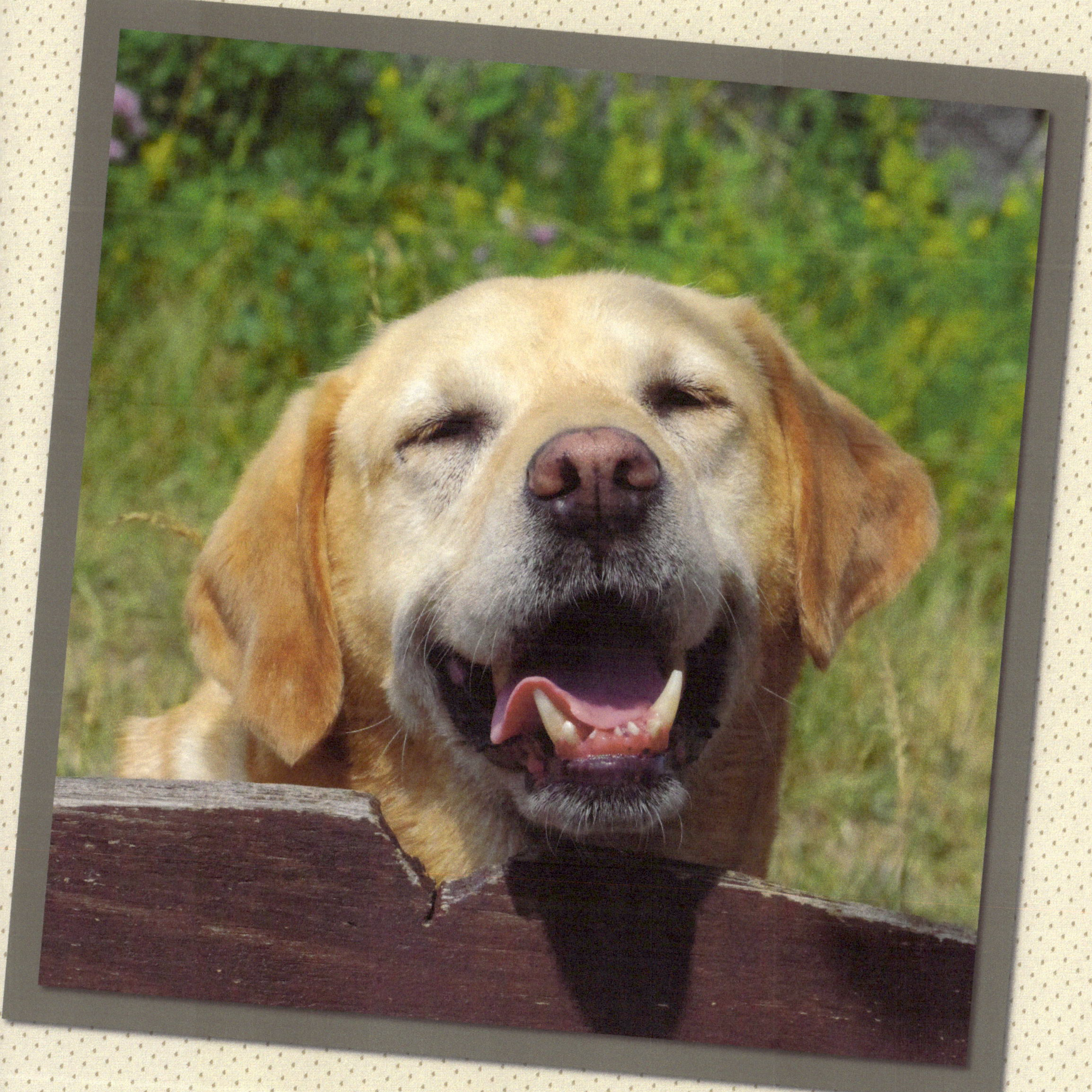

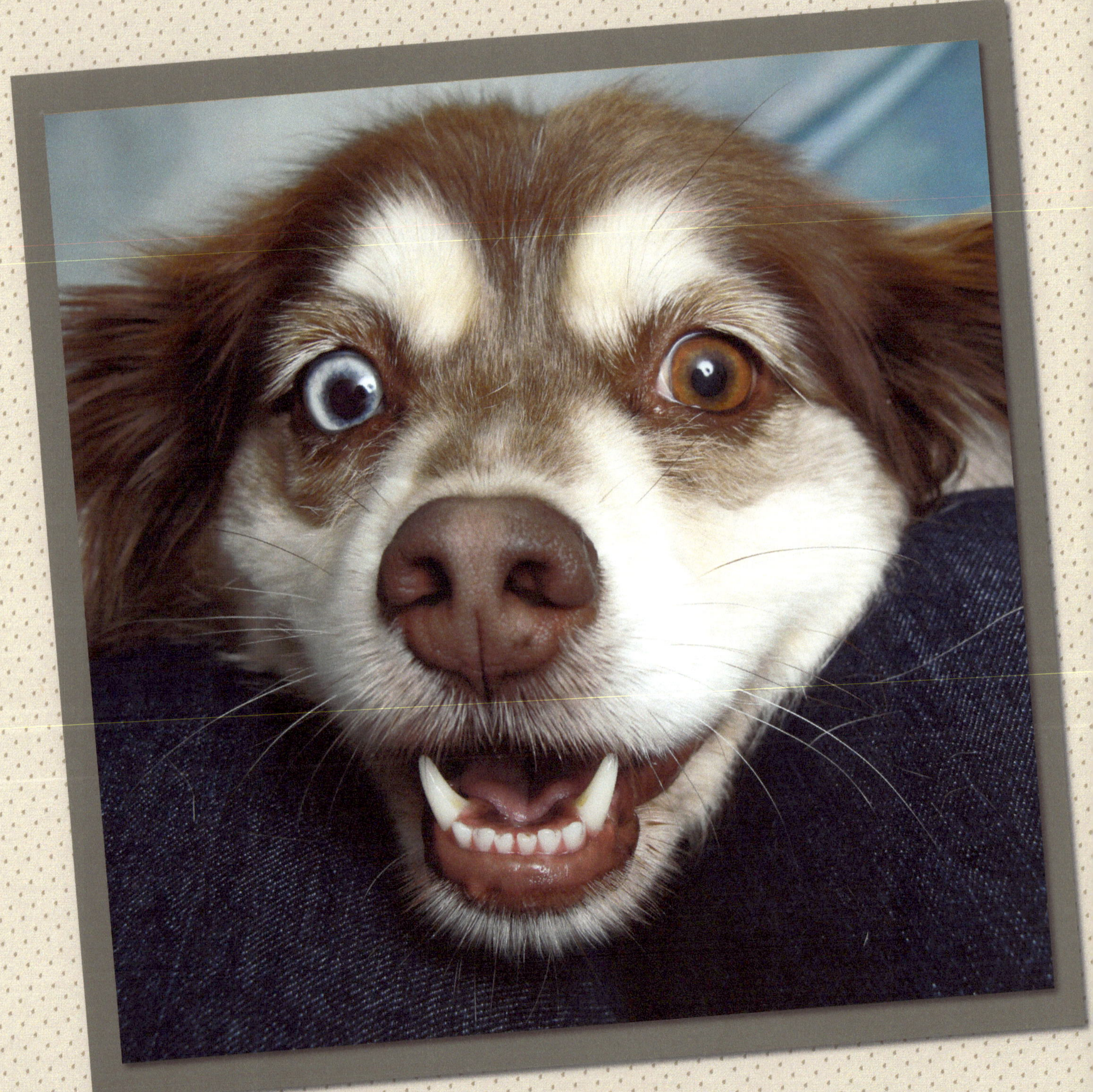

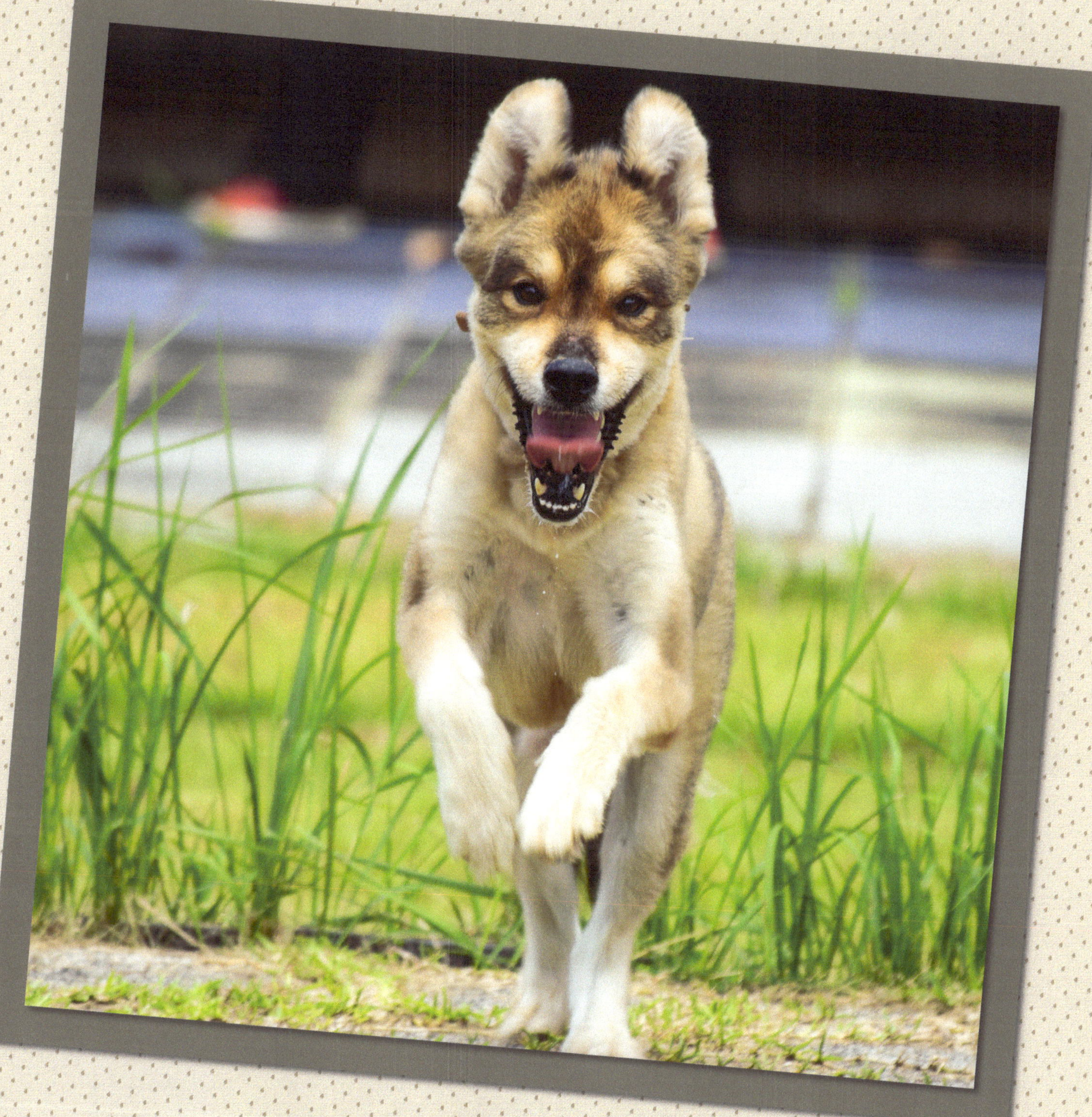

Thank You for Your Purchase from

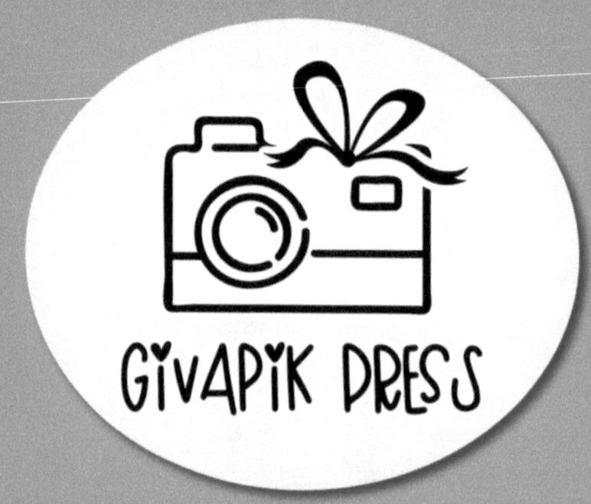

Please consider leaving a positive review for this book, it really helps small businesses!

For more fun gift books like this, please visit our Amazon author page:

Amazon.com/author/givapikpress